I0114910

The
Breath Of Life
And
The Flame Divine

By
Hilton Hotema

978-1-63923-481-3

Printed: October 2022

Cover Art By: Amit Paul

Published and Distributed By:
Lushena Books
607 Country Club Drive, Unit E
Bensenville, IL 60106
www.lushenabks.com

ISBN: 978-1-63923-481-3

THE BREATH OF LIFE

AND

THE FLAME DEVINE

Prof. Hilton Hotema

THE FLAME DIVINE

By Prof. Hilton Hotema.

Despots Love Darkness

1. Not long ago a vary great dootor wrote: "Our knowledge of man is still rudimentary. An endoorinologist, a psychoanalyst, a biologioal chemist, ere equally ignorant of man. Man oan be reduoed neither to a physioo-ohemioal system nor to a spiritual entity.

Unlike most dootors, this man was inspired by a unique impulse. He had little interest in disease, remedies, vaooines and serums,-- the staple wares of schools that produoe dootors who live and thrive on the miseries of man.

First of all, this dootor saw man as a god. He said: "Man stands above all things."

He oalled man's Mind the most oolossal power in this world, and then said: "The Mind is oompletely negleoted by physiologista and eoonomists, and almost unnotioed by physioians."

He said that in the study of Man we should investigate the qualities that make man what he is.

We oan know little about man as long as we negleot to study Mind, Consoiousness, Intelligenoe, and Vitality,--Those four inexplioable mysteries whioh oonstitute man, and oonoerning whioh science admits that it knows almost nothing.

One of the great soientists of modern times frankly deolared: "I oannot explain why I am alive rather than dead."

It is definitely dangerous for doctors to treat the siok until they know something about why man is e living being. And if that rule were observed, there would be no doctors qualified to attend a siok man.

After forty years of diligent research, this extraordinary dootor was ready to establish a sohool and teaoh the real Soienoe of Man --greatest of all soienoes.

Shooking! Theology and medioal art stood aghast. This must not be. Suoh knowledge would explode every theologioal dogma and destroy every medioal oonoept of disease.

So, in 1944, this good dootor met the fate that usually befalls those sinoere persons who would disseminate light in a floundering world. He was arrested on false oharges, put in prison, and there died suddenly of "heart attaok."

And onoe more theology and medioal art were saved, to continue exploiting the raoe; and man would oontinue to speoulate in darkness as to his origin, his ailments. and his end.

Meorooosm and Miorooosm

2. Creative Prooesses work from unity to diversity, from

-1-

center to circumference, from bud to bloom.

Primal Principles are invisible workers, and are responsible for all visible phenomena. Until we recognize that fact, we search in vain for the Secret of Life, and all speculations fail because they spring from false conceptions.

Causes are invisible powers; and Effects are visible products. Invisible Principles produce Visible Phenomena. Invisible vapor produces visible water.

The invisible powers of the Macrocosm produce the visible Microcosm, and the former is illustrated in the latter,---the one, of course, infinitely above the other. For Like begets Like in character, if not in degree.

The qualities, properties and attributes of the Microcosm are the epitomistic representations of the Macrocosm so completely and so perfectly, that the latter is manifest in the former, and vice versa.

CREATIVE ELEMENTS AND PRINCIPLES.

3.   Ancient Science postulated Four Creative Elements and Two Creative Principles.

The former are the four biblical Beasts symbolized in the Sphinx as Fire, Air, Water and Earth. The latter are the good and bad serpents of the Bible, and are represented by the White (Positive, Male) and the Black (Negative, Female) --Serpents of the Caduceus.

According to ancient science, the tetradical elements are the essence of created forms, and Polarity is the Power of Creative Processes. Without Polarity there would be no creation and no universe. The two Serpents represent the duadical powers of Polarity.

It becomes important to understand that the Four Creative Elements are interchangeable, being the tetradical phases of the Monad, the latter appearing as the Aeriferous Substance that surrounds the earth, and of which the earth is constituted not only, but all things thereon, called Nature, including Man.

FIRST PRINCIPLE.

4.   The Greek Philosopher Thales (640-546-BC) considered the universe a living organism, being the expression of a living force or "soul."

Aristotle (384-322-BC) said tha "soul" is diffused throughout the whole universe, and it may have been this conception that caused Thales to think all thing were full of "gods."

Anaximenes (380-320-BC) asserted that nothing in the universe is permanent but the First Principle, which is not only the cause of Matter and Motion, but is Matter and Motion combined.

Then he advanced the hypothesis that Air is that "First Principle."

Plutarch (46-120-AD) held that "All things are generated by a certain condensation and rarefaction of Air.

In the single surviving fragment of his writings, Anaximenes said: "Air is the nearest to an immaterial essence; for since we are generated in the flow of air, it is necessary that it be infinite and abundant. It is never exhausted nor diminished."

AEROLOGY.

5. A study of the Aeriferous Substance that surrounds the earth has been neglected in modern times because of its apparent unimportance and lack of pecuniary possibilities. Yet it is the Atmospheric Soil that contains the Virility of all Life.

It was not until 1766 when Joseph Priestly discovered "oxygen," and showed that air is not an "element" as science thought. but a complex mixture.

In 1784, Henry Cavendish produced water by exploding a mixture of hydrogen and oxygen,--thus somewhat revealing the nature of water. But its exact constitution is not yet known.

In 1920, Dr. N. R. Campbell, in his "Physics--The Elements," stated that, "We know far less about the constitution of water than about some organic compounds with a name a yard long."

William Prout (1785-1850), English physicist, is said to have been the first to divine the invisible gases from which all other elements are now believed to be built up, by the successive addition of one negative and one positive electron to each kind of atom.

AIR IS ALL.

6. In holding that Air is the First Principle, Anaximenes declared: "The Essence of the Universe is in the Infinite Air in eternal motion which contains ALL in itself."

According to Anaximenes, when exceedingly attenuated, air becomes fire; when more condensed, wind; a still further condensation produces clouds; greater compression changes clouds into water; further pressure produces the earth; and finally stones are formed as matter becomes still more condensed; these successive changes being produced by motion, which is constant.

He considered the Aeriferous Substance an animative essence, containing the Virility of all Life, and in continuous motion, thus incessantly changing its forms and generating new things,--things not contained, as such, in the primitive homogenous substance.

Force is the essence of the animative substance; hence Air, composed of the Four Elemente and the Two Creative Principles, automatically produces the world and all things therein.

Thus have all things been produced. and thus will be produced all things to come.

7.   We now approach a point in ancient philosophy concerning Man that is amazing for its simplicity and startling for its mysticity. It reveals the incessant trickery employed by the "powers that be" to keep the mases in mysterious darkness.

The mythical history of Freemasonry states that there once existed a WORD of surpassing value, and claiming a profound veneration; that the WORD was known to but few; that at length it was lost; and that a temporary substitute for it was adopted.

The Jews had a secret word,--the Tetragrammation, or four-lettered name, which all were forbidden to pronounce. It was always spelt, and expressed in four words, which represented the symbolical tatrad, exhibited in the temples of the Ancient Mysteries by the four forms of the Sphinx,--Man, Eagle, Lion, and Bull, the Four Beasts of the Bible; which corresponded with the Four Elements of the universe,--Fire, Air, Water and Earth.

This secret WORD was called the Ineffable Name, and was hidden in all the ancient sanctuaries. It represented the Four Elements which constitute Man when combined in one organic form.

For the purpose of confusion the Four Beasts (Sphinx), are given wild and sensational descriptions in the Bible, such as those appearing in Ezekiel, Chapter 1, vs. 4, 5, 15-21, and Daniel 7:107).

In Revelation the same four beasts appear; one like a Lion, one like a Calf, the third had a Man's face, and the fourth was like a flying Eagle. (4: 6, 7)

We are beginning to learn the reason why the Four Beasts (Sphinx) play such an important part in ancient scriptures.

CONSTITUTION OF MAN.

8.   The Four Beasts, the Four Elements symbolized by the Sphinx as Fire, Air, Water and Earth, we shall designate as astral, aerial, fluidal and material.

So, the Four Beasts are given an important place in ancient scriptures because they symbolize the Constitution of Man.

A pin cannot penetrate the flesh anywhere without drawing fluid from the body, composed of blood and lymph, and these are liquefied air.

Some think the lungs are the only part of the body containing air. Every part, every organ, every cell, all are interpenetrated by air.

The bony frame, the densest part of the body; is built by blood of blood, making the bones solidified blood, which is liquefied air.

These divisions combined constitute physical Man. They are composed of condensed air, which is composed of gases, which are composed of atoms, making the body an aggregation of atoms.

Engendering, sustaining, vitalizing, and informing these divisions is the work of the most powerful, most mysterious and most dangerous Force known, called by the Ancient Masters, THE FLAME DIVINE.

THE SACRED FIRE.

9.   "I sense one Flame, O Gurudeva; I see countless undetached sparks shining in it" (Secret Doctrine, Blavatsky.)

The Sacred Fire of the Ancient Masters symbolized The Flame Divine, the Great Philosophy of antiquity that now lies buried beneath the ruins of the Temples of the Ancient World.

In the humblest hut of the East there is always a light--a light that never fails, physically or symbolically.

A light constantly burns before the Holy Ark of the synagogue. There is one over the altar of the Church, and one illuminating the Crescent of the Mosque. In ancient days there was a light upon the hearth.

Fire Worship has its symbolical meaning, and is the oldest of all religious systems.

Pyra is Greek for Fire or Light that illuminates and heats. Midos is Greek and means "measures."

The word Pyramid comes from Pyra and Midos, and means "light-measures."

The great Pyramid of Gizeh, built fifty thousand years ago some claim, symbolized the Terrestrial Flame (the Microcosm), seeking ascension to and absorption in the Celestial Flame, the Macrocosm.

This most ancient doctrine was the Flame Secret of the Fire Worshippers.

FIRE.

10.   What makes a steam-engine move? Fire. What makes a gas-engine move? Fire. What makes an automobile move? Fire. What is lightning? Fire. What is electricity? Fire.

And according to the Bible, the God of the Jews was FIRE (Heb. 12:29).

What is Fire? Exceedingly attenuated AIR said Anaximenes (Sec. 6).

Ancient Science derived all things from Fire by rarefaction and condensation; the one active, the other passive, the one synthetic the other analytic.

Heraclitus (535-475-BC) considered all things as derived from Fire, and eventually transformed again into Fire.

The Pythagoreans regarded Fire as constituting the Heart of the

-5-

Universe, the Monad or First Form.

They regarded Fire as Extending from the earth to the limits of the Cosmos. All things were derived from Fire, and strive ever to return to Fire, the Eternal Flame Divine.

Clements of Alexandria said, "Fire, from the sun, is first changed to air, then to moisture, and from this came the earth also all things on it.

11. According to Ancient Astrology, the entire universe is "Fire in the process of transformation."

Ancient Science attributed to Fire a far wider connotation than it has for us,--Thanks to modern teaching that keeps the masses in darkness.

The Ancient Astrologers said, "From Fire to Earth and back again, an infinite number of worlds are born, only to suffer annihilation in due course, succeeded by reconstruction and redestruction without end."

They considered all solids were condensed Fire, only to be re-kindled in the process of universal transformation.

Fire constituted the flash of lightning, the burning flame of what we call combustion and heat.

They mentioned "the fiery ether," and the Atomists described "the fiery atoms."

Fire is the most ancient symbol of Life, and the greatest of all purifying agencies.

In the Egyptian Mysteries there was a symbolical purification of the neophyte by the Sacred Fire.

The Sacred Fire of the Ancient Astrologers was a symbol that concealed the meaning of one of their deepest secrets.

ASTRAL RAYS.

12. Atomic discoveries are leading back to the Astrological Age. Science calls it Cosmic Radiation. Ancient Science called it Astral Rays, and it was the foundation of their Science of Astrology.

There was a secret reason why Astrology has been condemned as the folly of the "star-mongers." Under the new name of Cosmic Radiation it is hailed as the discovery of the age.

Sir James Jeans, F.R.S., was one of the first of modern scientists to invite attention, a quarter of a century ago, to the impact of astral rays on man. He wrote:

"Cosmic radiation strikes the earth in large quantities. Every second it breaks up about 20 atoms in every cubic inch of our atmosphere and millions of atoms in our bodies, and we know not what the physiological effects may be."

Dr. R. A. Millikan, cosmic ray expert, wrote in 1935 that enormously energetic bullets (astral rays) from all directions strike the heads of mortals on the earth.

13. Prof. P. M. S. Blackett, F.R.S., stated in 1939 that "the earth is bombarded by atomic particles of surprisingly high energy."

Millikan said that cosmic rays contact the earth's magnetic field (aura) as electrons of more than 10 million volts, and penetrate more then 700 feet into the earth's crust. Some assert that certain rays pass entirely thru the earth.

Science did not consider it expedient to notice the effect of astral rays on man until 1939; and in 1940 a prominent British medical doctor admitted: "We hardly know anything about the effects of cosmic radiation on human beings."

Our smug science received a startling shook in 1939 when there appeared a book by George Lakhovsky, French scientist, titled "Secret of Life."

His work dealt inter alia with the effects of astral rays upon the body's cells and tissues; and what he said exploded so completely the scientific theory that Life "is the expression of a series of chemical changes in the body," that his book was highly obnoxious to medical art and had a hard time entering the U.S.A.

L I F E.

14. The masses look to science to solve the mystery of Life, and science admits thru the voice of its leaders that it is lost in the darkness.

Dr. R. A. Millikan, world renowned scientist, late head of the California Institute of Technology, authority on Cosmic Rays, said:

"I cannot explain why I am alive rather than dead. Physiologist can tell me much about the mechanical and chemical processes of my body, but why I am alive they cannot say" (Collier's, Oct. 24, 1925).

Then when Lakhovsky's "Secret of Life" appeared, translated from French by Mark Clements, the observations and conclusions advanced were so revolutionary, that they shocked leading scientists into cold silence, and were received with the same bitter scorn and chagrin that greeted Harvey's announcement in 1616 of his discovery of the circulation of the blood.

No doctor of that day who had reached the age of 40, ever acknowledged or accepted Harvey's discovery; and it will be many decades before medical art acknowledges and accepts Lakhovsky's philosophy as to the "Secret of Life."

ELECTRICITY.

15. Lakhovsky showed the body cell is composed of a nucleus containing chromosomes, surrounded by cytoplasm and a cell wall.

-7-

Chromosomes are composed of insulating material (lipods), filled with conducting fluid of a certain chemical composition. This organization forms an oscillating circuit of exceedingly small wavelength, capable of self-induction and capacity to vibrate at terrific speed, equivalent to that of Astral Rays.

He also showed that body cells are bipolar mechanisms, and chromosomes are tiny radio antennae, which pick up or receive Astral Radiation and convert it into vito-electric currents under the Astrological Law of Animation, thus formulating a Law of Psychology, Biology, ane Physiology.

And that is the secret of cellular activity, not chemical changes occurring in the body cells, as science erroneously claims.

We shall now anticipate slightly by observing that Astral Rays coursing thru the nerves, as electricity flows thru wires, produce the energization called Life, which makes Life a Product and not a Principle.

Then, what is Life? Just a state of corporeal activation result ing from Astral Rays flowing thru the nerve system of the body. The body is dead the moment that flow of force stops.

16. Anaximenes said that Air, the First Principle is Matter, and Motion combined. In more specific terms, that First Principle is Astro-Electro-Atomic Radiation.

The known processes and products of the Atom show that is possesses the tetradical properties of attraction, repulsion, sensation and volition.

These animatistic properties indicate the Atom possesses the quaternary qualities called Life, consisting of Vitality, Consciousness, Intelligence and Polarity.

The infinite products of the Atom show there are many kinds, and they build the multitudinous variety of phenomena that cover the earth with what is called the mineral, vegetal and animal kingdoms.

It is proven by demonstration that the Atom possesses terrific power,--astro-electricity.

The purpose of the power of the Atom is constructive work according to law, which evidence indicates that Atoms possess Consciousness to do work, Mental Ability to perform the task, and Cosmic Intelligence to do the work according to antecedent plan and pattern.

These properties and attributes of the Atom pass into the body cells the Atoms build, and into the organ and glands, brain and nerves.

The Atom exhibits properties which place it on the plane of Mind, solving the secret of Cosmic Mind and Cosmic Consciousness, --qualities which theology claims for its anthropomorphic God.

Atomic power, mind, consciousness, and intelligence. Tha secret of the ages possessed by the Atom, all overlooked and unrecognized because theology teaches that these properties are the attributes of its God, then destroys the ancient scriptures so the world would never know the facts.

Thomas A. Edison, noted inventor, said Atoms are entities which live forever, and to that extent at least the Eternal Life for which we hope is a reality,--all governed by law and not by faith and belief.

THE ARCHEUS

17. There is a twisted and distorted statement in the Bible as follows: "For we know that if our earthly house of this tabernacle were dissolved, we have a building of God, an house not made with hands, eternal in the heavens" (2 Cor. 5:1).

From the Aeriferous Substance surrounding the earth springs the visible world called Nature,--the visible product of the invisible principle.

All material phenomena originate in the Aeriferous Substance, and involution of the cosmic pattern precedes evolution of the material product.

The Archetype of visible phenomena pre-exists in the Aeriferous Substance as the Cosmic Model of that which appears, being the directing agency of the Formative Forces in the production of Symmetrical Forms.

Prof. Hotema says in "Pre-Existence of Man" that the Supreme Entity on earth is Man, and he is logically the Divine Archeus in the Aeriferous Substance from which creative processes unfold his visible body.

It is the Divine Archeus that is referred to in the Bible as "an house not made with hands, eternal in the heavens."

The Processes of Creation occur not only around us in the Macrocosm, but also within us,--the Microcosm.

Creation was the Biological Drama of the Ancient Masters in which are involved all Cosmic Principles and Cosmic Elements, and which Drama was so skilfully presented in the Ancient Mysteries to the neophyte in his initiation, and so cleverly concealed from the eyes of the world in the Science of Astrology.

18. Ancient Science held that material forms on earth rise from the immaterial essence of the Aeriferous Substance,--the doctrine of Archetypes or Telarche.

Dr. Gustaf Stromberg, noted astronomer, presented in "Soul of The Universe" a postulate of creative processes which he demonstrated to be sound.

He declared that in the Aeiferous Substance surrounding the earth, there are whirling vortexes which determine structure and function of living bodies.

Then he proved by experiments that the Immaterial Archeus does lie back of the material formation.

With a super-sensitive instrument he explored the electrical field in the water surrounding a tadpole. As the animal passed thru the transformative stage from tadpole to frog, the effect was start-ling.

This test proved that the Immaterial Essence of the future animal does exist as the Archeus in the Aeriferous Substance before it appears in the visible state.

Unknowable Reality

19. The mystery of Life led Ancient Science into all phases of biological research.

The perplexing enigma down thru the ages has been, What is Life? What animates the body?

Is it Food? No. Water? No. Is it Air? That must be the answer, for when man stops breathing he stops living. Not only that, but as soon as Air leaves the body, said Diogenes, "then life, mind, consciousness and intelligence disappear."

With the haystack right before us, the prospects look promising. Now, all we have to do is to find the needle. Ancient Science found it, but modern science has not.

The world's greatest scientists overtly admit thay cannot ex-plain why man is a living being.

Wisdom alone bestows sufficiency; but wisdom is empty when it fails to solve the Secret of Life.

After studying man for forty years, the great Dr. Alexis Carrel was unable to define Life. He wrote:

"We do not apprehend man as a whole. We know him as composed of distinct parts; and even these parts are created by our methods. Man is composed of a procession of phantoms, in the midst of which there strides an Unknowable Reality" (Man The Unknown, 1935, p. 4).

20: Carrel made no definite attempt to analyze his "Unknowable Reality," but rather to emphasize, by his silence, the impression that it was beyond the capacity of man to describe.

He did condemn in acrimonious tones what he termed "the childish physico-chemical conceptions" of Life, "in which so many physiologist and physicians still believe" (p. 108). But he presented nothing to replace these "childish conceptions."

Herbert Spencer, renowned evolutionist of the 19th century, re-garded Life as just a mode of motion. He wrote:

"The broadest and most complete definition of Life will be the continuous adjustment of internal relations to external relations."

If Life means only motions, the word does not mean what the masses think it means. The word is descriptive and not attributive. Automobiles move, but they are not alive.

The specific qualities of Life are Consciousness, Mind, Intelligence and Action. Automobiles possess only the last, and science makes no attempt to explain how the other three emanate from physico-chemical processes.

What Is Life

21. We are beginning to realize that the term Life means not all the world believes it means.

As we have previously shown, the word Life is a misleading term (15). It is regarded as an entity, a principle. That erroneous assumption is responsible for the confusion surrounding the word.

Living bodies possess power of movement. So do automobiles. But living bodies also possess consciousness, mind and intelligence, --qualities not found in automobiles.

Does the difference lie in the nature of the motivating power, or the mechanism?

A live wire is one charged with electricity. When the charge is absent, the wire is dead. The analogy between a living body and a live wire should lead to surprising results.

The Fiery Man

22. We have said that Fire was the most ancient symbol of Life, and that Fire furnishes the motivative power of modern mechanisms.

We shall see that Fire makes Man a Living Soul (Solar Man) on the earth plane; and that the remarkable difference between living bodies and moving automobiles lies not so much in the nature of the power as in the nature of the mechanism.

Watch and see how readily and how easily we discover Solar Man.

A pin cannot be pressed against the body any where without touching a Nerve; and Nerves are charged, in Life, with what science calls Nerve Force.

For this force science has no definite name nor explanation. It is just "food energy," or the result of "chemical action" in the body or "a series of chemical changes occurring in the cells," as the great Osler said.

We have found the darkness in which doctors get lost. But if any medical doctor questions or attacks that theory of life in public, he very summarily has his license as a physician revoked on the charge of "unethical conduct." Doctors must stay in line or get out. That doctrine blocks progress.

Man would be amazed if he could see in its entirety the Nerve System of his body. For it would present to the eye the same size, shape and form of the dense physical body.

The Nerve System of vito-electrical wires constitutes the Living Flame on earth. The wires are interlaced, interwoven and interblended so completely and so perfectly with the physical body, that in our sight the Flame Divine and the physical form of man appear as one.

When we gaze in a mirror, we see only the physical form, little suspecting that we are actually looking at Eternal Solar Man.

And once more the facts prove that Truth is stranger than Fiction.

23.   And so, at long last the discredited and condemned Astrological Age has returned.

The facts are forcing modern science into the Astrological Age, to the consternation of theology and medical art.

For the Astrological Age takes us back to the Ancient Wisdom, to the Sphinx, which symbolizes the Four Elements, to the Caduceus, which symbolizes the Two Creative Principles, to Pyramid, which symbolizes the Terrestrial Flame Divine seeking ascension to the Celestial Flame Divine, to the God of the Jews, who symbolized a Consuming Fire (Hebrews 12:29).

The great discoveries of Lakhovsky, in the realm of radiation, gave the modern world, for the first time, a sound Law of Animation. He showed that what is called Life is actually a state of activation resulting from Astral Rays flowing thru the nerves of the body as electrical currents.

As Fire makes an automobile move, so Fire makes man's body move.

Lakhovsky further showed that cellular activity is the effect of Astral Rays converted into vito-electrical currents and conveyed by the nerves to all parts of the body.

The discoveries of Lakhovsky changes the status of Life from a suppositional Entity to a condition of activity in the body,--a mode of motion as Spencer said.

As man makes and directs pilotless planes and controls his missiles by radar rays, he is actually copying Creative Processes by which he himself is produced, vitalized, intelligized, and controlled.

Some advanced physiologists have discovered that each cell of the body is a complete, bipolar, electrical mechanism; while the organism as a whole is an intricate, electrical machine, composed of billions of batteries,

Macrocosmic Generator

24.   Electricity is an eternal, elemental force, the exact nature of which is still undetermined.

Our local Sun is the giant generator that supplies the earth with most of its electricity.

We think our Sun is large, and so it is compared to our earth; but the red giant, Antares, is some hundred of thousands of times larger; and the brightest star (sun) now known, is S. Doredus, is 500,000 times brighter.

If this giant sun replaced our local Sun, the planet Jupiter, about 470,000,000 miles from our Sun, would be inside of the star.

Because of the earth's protective screen of Aeriferous Substance man is shielded from the ripping rays flowing from these giant generators.

The Microcosmic Battery

25. Revelation, Book of Sevens, great book of the Bible, compiled from the dusky scrolls of India as shown by Hotema in his "Son of Perfection," is a scripture that describes, in symbol and allegory, the principal battery of the body, with its Seven Master Cells, and also the Seven Sensual Powers of the brain which make Men a Master when these Seven Cells are fully activated as they should be.

The body's main electric battery has seven chief cells, and when the seven cells are energized as they were in early, undegenerate men, the seven sensory powers come into action and exalt Man to the plane of Seership.

The ancient scriptures said: "The evidence of activation is the Power of Seership."

The biblical makers distorted that statement and made it read: "The testimony of Jesus is the spirit of prophecy" (Rev. 19:10).

Each cell of the body's chief battery controls its part of the body, indicated in the Bible by seven cities, each noted for some product that draws attention to that part of the body.

For instance, the generative region of the body is indicated by Smyrna, noted for its fig industry. The fig is preeminently a phallic symbol.

The Bible says, "And the eyes of both were opened, and they knew they were naked; and they sewed fig-leaves together, and made themselves aprons"(Gen. 3:7).

To each city mentioned in Revelation was sent a message, indicating the nature and function of each cell. A certain aspect of the Flame Divine was presented, a good and evil quality ascribed, and a prize promised, specifying the astral benefits accruing to "The Conquerer" (man) from the conquest (activation) of each of the seven cells.

Revelation is the greatest work of symbol allegory that man ever produced; and the ancient Astrologers who wrote it were far ahead of us in the field of Astral Radiation.

THE DEADLY POWER.

26. What we call Electricity is the most powerful and most mysterious force known. It has its good and evil aspects, the results produced depending upon the conditions supplied.

Its work is limited only by the mechanism thru which it operates It heats water and freezes it, turns wheels and luminates globes, runs clocks and rings bells. And it animates animal bodies and executes them.

Two doctors, working on radar development during World War II, made a killing discovery that just leaked out.

In ten seconds a technician standing in the invisible ray of a radar transmitter, felt uncomfortable sensations of heat in his abdomen; in less than a minute the intensity of the heat made him move out of range.

Within two weeks the men died. The surface of his body showed no marks, but an examination of the interior revealed that "his insides were cooked," said the doctors.

They reported that "a hole as large as a silver dollar was burned in the man's small bowel."

Soler Explosions

27. The discovery of the deadly effect of invisible radar rays caused some scientists to assert that this force is the destructive phase of the Life Ray. They point out that sun-rays are constructive and destructive, depending on conditions, and that all natural forces have their good and evil qualities.

We repeat that if it were not for the protective shield of Aeriferous Substance by which the earth is surrounded, all things on it would be destroyed by atomic particles shooting from the sun.

In addition to the regular rays flowing from the sun, giant explosions occur on its surface, sending out radioactive bursts of atomic particles that hit the earth within 18 to 36 hours.

Two such explosions recently occurred. It was estimated that in one of them a billion tons of the sun's gases were expelled as a huge bubble that roared out at 700 miles per second,--equal in power to thousands of H-bombs exploding simultaneously, and disrupting short-wave communication around the earth, creating vivid auroral displays, garbling radio teletype, and causing terrific disturbances in the earth's aura.

Creation.

28. Lightning, the active phase of astro-electricity, causes the formation of free oxygen in the air, thus serving a useful purpose for man.

An electric current sent thru a vessel of hydrogen and oxygen, two invisible gases, causes an explosion, followed by the formation of water; and there is not the slightest parity between the passive and active properties of the water and those of the hydrogen and oxygen gases that formed the water.

When electric circuit is disconnected, a spark of fire jumps the gap between the terminals. That spark is electrical and not something which burned between the terminals.

An electron is said to be the unit of energy of an electrical discharge. Lightning is said to be electrons in transit. The word "lightning" comes from electron.

Creation: Astro-electro-magnetic forces constitutes the Aeriferous Substance that surrounds the earth, end the countless numbers of invisible rays, proceeding from this Atmospheric Soil, produces all visible phenomena on earth, including the vegetal end animal kingdoms.

The Conscious Soul

29. Beyond question we have reached the crux of the Mystery of Man. What we say may make scientists sneer in public, but study in private, while priests and preachers will shout that we do not understand the Bible.

It is common knowledge that vegetation is attached to the earth, but who suspects it is also attached to the Atmospheric Soil surrounding the earth?

We know that animals are bound to the earth by a force called gravity, but who ever dreamed they are bound to the Atmospheric Soil by a beam in which they live and move and have their being?

Science may scorn the postulate that man's nerve system serves the same purpose that the ignition system serves an automobile. But the scorn of science is the proof of the postulation.

Without fire in the ignition system, the automobile is dead. Without fire in the nerve system, the body is dead. That is a fact of demonstration. No guess-work about it.

In both cases the fire rises from electricity, but different in nature.

The one is produced by a man-made generator and battery; the other by Astral Bodies.

The supply of the former is limited; that of the latter is infinite.

The former is a blind force; the latter is the Conscious Soul of the Universe.

Rarefaction and Condensation.

30. The earth spins on its axis, from west to east, at 1040 miles per hour. If man were not held to it by a strong magnetic force, he would be flung off violently into space.

Man is also bound by electro-magnetic force to the Aeriferous

Substance that surrounds the earth.

We have said that when man directs pilotless planes and controls speeding missiles with radar rays, he copies Creative Processes by which he is produced, animated and controlled.

The air which science formerly regarded as being so empty, is found to be filled with everything that materializes on earth, as taught by the Ancient Astrologers, who held that visible objects are composed of condensed Air, and declared that Air is Matter and Motion combined.

The late Thomas A. Edison, noted inventor, had a plant in which he condensed nitrates from the air. The substance was sacked and sold to farmers for fertilizer.

In 1953, two Canadian doctors demonstrated by test that the leaves of sugar beets change air into cellulose in ten seconds.

Lead, a metallic substance, when put in a pot on a hot stove, soon boils away and floats as gas in the air.

These and many other cases and incidents demonstrate that Air is Matter and Motion combined.

Chiropractic

31. Man makes metal wires to convey electricity, thus copying cosmic processes.

His own body has "wires" that receive and convey astro-electricity to all parts and organs of his body. The wires are nerves which form the Flame Divine, the Solar Man (15, 22).

No system of caring for the sick has ever grown so fast as Chiropractic has. That amazing growth is due to the fact that it is based on sound principles, while medicine has none.

Chiropractic deals with the Nerve System, the Flame Divine. Medicine deals with changeable symptoms, and changes treatment as the symptoms change.

When Chiropractic Schools were first founded little more than half a century ago, they had to use medical text-books. These books were so deficient as to the brain and nerves, that they were discarded and replaced with books prepared by leading Chiropractors.

The medical trust tries various diabolical tricks to crush Chiropractic because of its grand success.

Chiropractors are arrested on false charges of "practicing medicine without a license," when the real reason is getting the sick well after the sufferers were abandoned as incurable by able medical doctors.

This attitude of medical art shows that the sick are supposed to die for the glory of medicine if they do not respond to regular medical treatment.

Biblical Symbology.

32. It is now in order to observe some strange symbology of the Ancient Astrologers that appears in the Bible, which means little to the multitude but much to the esoteric. These Symbols represent certain points which we are discussing in the mystery of Man.

The first is the Silver Cord; the second, Jacob's Ladder; and the third, a trap door in the sky.

1. Or ever the Silver Cord be loosed, or the Golden Bowl be broken (Eccl. 12:6).

2. And Jacob dreamed, and behold a ladder set up on the earth and the top if it reached to heaven: and the angels (were) ascending and descending on it (Gen. 28:12).

3. After this I looked, and, behold, a door (was) opened in heaven (Rev. 4:1).

The exoteric never dream that this strange symbolism conceals from the eyes of the world, certain creative processes of the Macrocosm, and definite animative functions of the Microcosm.

We must be made to realize that man's relation to the universe is forever fixed by the fact that his body is constituted of vibrating atoms, cosmic in character and combined in form by cosmic polarity.

The Silver Cord

33. The Nerve System, we said, constitutes the Living Flame on earth (22).

We have now come to a strange secret. The nerves, say medical books, begin in the brain and end in various parts and organs of the body.

If that were true, vitality, consciousness, mind and intelligence would be the greatest of all miracles.

These are the qualities of Life, and these are such a puzzle to our smug science, that no concerted effort is made to analyze them. There seems to be no place to begin. Great scientists frankly admit that they cannot define Life nor explain why they are alive (14.)

Now, if the nerves do begin in the brain, whence comes the power called "nerve force," which science says makes all parts of the body function and the heart to beat?

No sound, sensible, logical answer to that question cen be found in all the medical books on earth.

Science knows little about the nerves and nothing about the essence of "nerve force."

The nerves just begin in the brain, and mind, consciousness, intelligence, vitality and nerve force originate in the brain. From what?

These qualities which constitute Life just seem to spring out of nothing, or to rise from internal chemical action.

35. The nerves appear to begin in the brain, but do not. The sun seems to rise, but does not. The earth seems to be stationary, but is not.

When Dr. Hervey shocked the medical world in 1616 with the announcement of his discovery of the circulation of the blood in the body, he could not determine how the blood passes from the arteries to the veins, as no connecting tubes could be seen by the aid of the best microscope then available.

Hervey knew the blood passes from the arteries to the veins, but could not explain the mystery. The arteries seemed to end in nothing and the veins to begin in nothing. Just as the nerves seem to begin from nothing in the brain.

Medical ert, learning nothing from thet experience, says the nerves begin in the brain, converge at the Medulla Oblongata portion of the brain, end there form the spinal cord, which extends down the spine, with nerves branching from it and going all over the body.

Ancient Science knew that the nerves could not begin in the brain; for the nerves are charged with the Fiery Force that does not originate in the brein, but in the Aeriferous Substance which surrounds the earth.

The nerves seem to begin in the brain because their real beginning is invisible.

36. Now grasp this shocking secret--the Nerves begin as Astral Rays.

The Astral Rays of the Aeriferous Substance converge es the Silver Cord at the Fonticulus Frontalis (door opened in heaven) in the crown of the heed (Golden Bowl), and there transform end condense into materiel fibers, to become the visible beginnings of the nerves, The Soler Body on earth.

As the leaves of beets change astral rays into cellulose (30), so the brain tissues more readily change Astral Reys into nerve fibers.

The visible portion of the nerves does begin in the brain; and that part consists of Astral Reys that are invisible beams until materialization changes them into visible fibers.

Nerve-beginnings in the brain present an analogy to the beginnings of the veins in the body.

Hervey could not see the beginnings of the veins by the aid of his microscope; and no microscope now available can reveal the beginnings of the nerves in the brain.

Neither could any microscope make visible the deadly beam that killed in less than a minute, a man who stood in its range and had his insides cooked (26).

Cosmic Rhythm

37. In the formative stage of the embryo, the brain forms first

The skull area where the Silver Cord penetrates the Golden Bowl is the Fonticulus Frontalis. To this important fontanel no medical books pay any especial attention. If it has a particular purpose, medical art knows it not.

In the skull there are seven fontanels. This one is much the largest remains open for a considerable time after birth, and present a rhythmic pulsation that accords with the heart's beet.

We are now at the core of the Flame Divine that flows from the Aeriferous Substance into the body. This Marcrocosmic Current which contains the Virility of all Life and flows into the brain end body as the Silver Cord, is that cosmic force for which medical art has vague theories but no sensible explanation.

Whence comes the force responsible for the psychologicel, biological, and physiological processes of the body? Whence come the inexplicable qualities of vitality, mind, consciousness, and intelligence?

Medical art has no answer for these questions. They may come from the brain, or perhaps from the food one eats.

That ridiculous system of speculation and theorization is called "medical science."

The Ancient Astrologers taught that the astro-electrical force of the Macrocosm is the power responsible not only for the heart's action, but for all function end pulsation of the body, including the life-qualities of vitality, consciousness, mind end intelligence

And this Ancient Wisdom of the Masters is all cleverly concealed from the eyes of the world in the ingenious symbolism of the Zodiakos of antiquity.

The Microcosm is of and from the Macrocosm, and the rhythmic pulsation and properties of the Macrocosm are those manifest in the Microcosm.

Doctors wonder as they witness the rhythms of cosmic force, but see not that those same rhythms appear in all physical processes of the body, nor realize that they are the expressions of that vito-electro-essence of the Macrocosm which make the Microcosm e Living Soul.

The Life Link.

38. The Silver Cord can be appropriately compared to the umbilical cord that links the unborn child to its mother. For it link the Microcosm to the Macrocosm.

We should regard the Silver Cord as analogous to a radio beam that extends for miles into the ether, and along which airplanes may be guided accurately and safely.

Doctors have reported many cases of patients undergoing operations, who leave the body and look down on the unconscious shell.

In such cases the complete Entity,--vitality, consciousness, mind and intelligence, is evulsed from the physical shell, and yet remains united to it by the Silver Cord, by means of which the Ego can return to and reactivate the shell,--provided the cord is not broken.

The Silver Cord is composed of Astral Rays and capable of infinite extension. In sleep we may, as in dreams, leave the body thru the trap door in the top of the Golden Bowl and fly miles away. The body remains alive and we return to it as long as the Silver Cord remains intact. But when it breaks, somatic death results.

The Ego.

39. The time will come when Chiropractic Schools will know and teach that the Silver Cord and the Spinal Cord are actually one, just a continuation of each other, the visible portion in the visible body, and the invisible portion in the Aeriferous Substance.

At the lower end of the spinal portion of the cord in the visible body, is the creative power of the Microcosm in the visible world; and at the upper end of the cord, in the Aeriferous Substance, is the creative power of the Macrocosm.

This esoteric secret of the Silver Cord and Jacob's Ladder was always closely guarded by the Ancient Masters, and heavily veiled in all ancient scriptures.

When man rises from his present low level of degeneration, and increases his common five sensory powers to the very rare Seven, symbolically mentioned many times in the Bible, then the Ego, while still attached to the somatic body by the Silver Cord, rises superior to the earth plane, leaves the body as in dreams, soars to the fourth dimensional plane, and for that period of time man is omniscient.

40. This is a rare state of life that will never be experienced by the multitude.

It is one of the strange secrets taught in the neophyte in the Ancient Mysteries.

One of the objects of initiation was to teach the neophyte how to liberate his reel self, the Ego, from his body.

These cases ere mentioned in the Bible in guarded terms, as "immediately I was in the spirit" (Rev. 1:10; 4:2).

No one was accepted for initiation until long investigation showed one to be worthy of the honor and the great power thus conferred upon one.

For this biological secret puts such power in the hands of the Initiate, that it would have been dangerous to society for it to be possessed by iniquitous, vicious persons.

It was the extraordinary care employed in screening applicants for admission that caused the final downfall of these great schools.

When Constantine the Great applied for admission and was rejected, his anger constrained him to start that movement which finally led to the destruction of these ancient institutions.

The work of destruction was consummated in the reign of Theodosius near the close of the fourth century.

That fatal blow to the great schools of antiquity started the course that finally led to the Fall of Rome, and sank Europe into a dungeon of darkness that lasted longer than a thousand years.

People today think the Dark Ages are gone. They are asleep. Their boasted liberty and enlightenment are largely imaginary. They can not miss what they never had.

41. The Flame Divine, the Solar Man, originates in the Aeriferous Substance, descends to the earth in the Silver Cord, and enters the body thru the "door opened in heaven," filling the body with all the qualities called Life.

The Flame Divine is symbolized in the Bible as the angel descending on Jacob's Ladder, and the process is called Birth.

In due course the Flame Divine leaves the body thru the same "door," and returns to its home in the Aeriferous Substance in which it lives and moves and has its being.

In this case the Flame Divine is symbolized as the angel ascending on Jacob's Ladder, and the process is called Death. The Bible calls it "born again" (Jn. 3:3,5,7).

The ascension of the Flame Divine to its home in the Aeriferous Substance is governed by the same law that rules in the descent of the Flame Divine to the physical body on earth.

For a split second at the moment of death, the Flame Divine can see the physical body while the objective consciousness is fading from material brain, and changing to Cosmic Consciousness of the Solar Body.

This change in the state of consciousness the biblical Paul termed, a Mystery. He said:

"Behold, I show you a mystery: We shall not sleep, but we shall be changed, in a moment, in the twinkling of an eye, ...and the dead shall be raised incorruptible, and we shall be changed. For this corruptible must put on incorruption, and this mortal must put on immortality" (1 Cor. 15:51-53).

There is no mystery about it when the facts are correctly pre-

-21-

sented.

Man's body is bound to the earth by the force called gravity; and by the Silver Cord the Flame Divine is attached to the Aeriferous Substance of the Astral World.

Man Is King.

42. The Virility of all Life is contained in the Aeriferous Substance surrounding the Earth, and is created by Astral Rays meeting and mixing with the Earth's Aura.

Astral Rays are the Positive Element, and the Earth's Aura forms the Negative Element. In these elements inheres the property of Polarity.

In the Aeriferous Substance dwells the eternal Archeus, or primal element of subjective objectivity, from which rise the tetradical qualities of Vitality, Consciousness, Mind and Intelligence. These combined constitute Life. They emanate from the Aeriferous Substance and they leave the body with the last breath.

Diogenes said that Life, Mind, Consciousness and Intelligence are properties of the Air, the First Principle. He stated:

"No sooner does Air leave the body, than these properties disappear. As all things arise from Air, to Air must all things return."

A great doctor has said that "man stands above all things on earth."

Man is King of the Universe. In him are recapitulated all animalculistic formations,--a fact employed by Evolutionists to support their empirical theory that Man is only an improved Ape.

Man is an improved Ape and More. He is the perfect embodiment of all living formations below him and above him, from the fish of the sea to the stars of the sky; and his Supreme Intelligence elevate; him to the exalted plane of the Flame Divine, with dominion over all things on earth.

That statement is supported by the ancient scriptures which were included in the Bible by the biblical makers.

Man has dominion over the fish of the sea, and the fowl of the air, and the cattle, and over all the earth (Gen. 1:26).

That King of the Earth needs no help from anything upon the earth. If man lived according to that law, he would not be wallowing in the mire where we find him. He looks to the church to "save his soul," and to the doctors to save his body. Little does he know that these have nothing for him.

Astrology.

43. Thales said the Soul of the Universe is an unsubstantial form of force, always in motion, and endows all things with action. He called it Soul for lack of a better term. Some say it is the Conscious Soul of the Cosmos.

Ancient Science, ages before Thales, called it Astral Radiation. It was the foundation of the Science of Astrology, the oldest and the greatest science in the world.

The beginnings of Astrology are unknown. The science emerges already highly refined from the dark obscurity of the pre-historic world.

The resurrection of this science will lift man up to an intellec tual and social status far above the limitations of our present con- sciousness. But that resurrection will never come so long as it can be prevented by theology; for it would reveal the astrological nature of Catholic-Christianity, so clearly shown in the works of Prof. Hotema.

In the British Journal of Astrology appeared the following attri bute:

"The best testimony to the truth of Astrology is that it has never halted, but has come undeviatingly down thru the ages, out of the mist of time, thru the ancient world and the mediaeval night of horror, to our present time."

Astrology goes much farther back than the "plains of Chaldea."

The Zodiakos.

44. Prof. Hilton Hotema shows in his Mystery Men of the Bible, to the amazement of the multitude, that the gospel Jesus is a per- sonification of an Astrological Symbol.

The gospel scribe made his Jesus say:

"In my Father's house are many mansions; if it were not so, I would have told you. I go to prepare a place for you. And if I go and prepare a place for you, I will come again, and receive you unto myself; that where I am, there ye may be also" (Jn. 14:2,3).

The "mansions" are the twelve symbols of the Zodiac. Jesus here represents the head sign of the Zodiac, Aries, and he is presented as addressing the other symbols of the Zodiac.

The Constellation of Aries was called the Lamb of God by the ancients, and also the Savior which taketh away the sins of the world.

When the Sun began its trend southward, people north of the equa tor knew that shorter days, longer nights, cloudy weather, barren fields, storms and cold were coming. This knowledge made them sad.

To them, the Sun was the regulator of mandene events, was the God of Light, of the Earth, of the Seasons, of the Harvest, of the People. They said "our God is a consuming Fire" (Ex. 24:17; Deut. 4:24; Ps. 50:3; Heb. 12:29, etc.).

Without the Sun, all were lost. So the ancient Egyptian and other races rejoiced and celebrated when the Sun, on reaching its farthest point in its southward journey, seemed to stop and begin to ascend after the winter solstice, apparently struggling against the malign influence of Aquarius and Pisces, while amicably received by Aries, Ram or Lamb, as "he, the Lamb of God, opened the equinox and saved the world from the wintry reign of cold and darkness."

This ancient celebration of the Sun and Aries was changed by the church to Christ-mas, and instead of the celebration's being in honor of the birth of the Sun of God, it was changed to the "birth of the only begotten Son of God."

The earth entered the zodiac sign of Aries in 2,433 B.C., and the cycle extended to 273 B.C., when the cycle of Pisces began.

During the 2160 years the earth was in the cycle of Aries, the Lamb of God was an object of great adoration. And a Lamb appeared on the Christian Cross until the year AD 680, which clearly indicated the origin of Catholic-Christianity and its Christ.

In that year the Sixth Ecumenical Council of Constantinople finally ordained, after a long and bitter debate, that in place of the Lamb, the figure of a man should be portrayed on the cross.

And that disposes of the gospel Jesus.

The statement "I will come again," is true and correct when properly understood and applied.

During each Grand Cycle of 25,920 years, our earth passes thru the twelve houses of the Zodiakos, just as our Sun goes thru them in a trifle over 365 days.

So, what was regarded as the birth of the Sun occurs in a new zodiacal sign every 2160 years. This brings the Lamb of God back every 25,960 years, reigning each time for 2160 years.

And that disposes of the second coming of Christ.

The secret of the gospel Jesus is based on the Science of Astrology; for which very good reason Astrology was condemned by the church, and all astrological records were destroyed.

(THE END)

-24-

THE BREATH OF LIFE.

Pert One.

Who can tell us what Life is? We must remain in darkness until we know.

We look to science for help, and science fails us. Greet scientists are as deeply in the dark over the Mystery of Life es the men in the street.

Alexis Carrel, on of the greatest of our time, wrote:

"Man is made up of a procession of phantoms, in the midst of which there strides an Unknowable Reality" (Man The Unknown, p.4).

The lete Dr. Robert A. Milliken, termed "the generalissimo of American Science in World War I," declared:

"I cannot explain why I am alive rather than dead. Physiologists can tell me much about the mechanical and chemical processes of my body, but they cannot say why I am alive" (Collier's, Oct. 24, 1925).

If we search back thru the literature of the last 2000 years, we find nothing to help us.

Hippocrates (460 B.C.), called the "Father of Medicine," said Life is "A flame burning in water."

Bichet said Life is "The sum of the functions by which death is resisted."

Spencer said Life is "The continuous adjustment of internal relations to external relations."

William Osler, termed the greatest doctor America ever produced, said Life is "The expression of a series of chemical changes."

And Carrel celled Life "An Unknown Reality."

The controlled press of the nation carries false propaganda designed to make men believe that "science is remaking our lives," while the bald facts tell a far different tale.

The great Carrel wrote:

"In fact, our ignorance (of the body and its functions) is profound."

"The functions of the most complex organs of the body still remain unknown."

"The science of man is the most difficult of all sciences."

"Our knowledge of the body is most rudimentary. It is impossible for the present, to grasp its constitution. We must, then, be content with the scientific observation of our organic and mental activities, and, without any other guide, march forward into the unknown.

"An endocrinologist, a psychoanalyst, a biological chemist, are equally ignorant of man...Our knowledge of man is still rudimentary... Most of the great problems...remain unsolved" (Man the Unknown).

In the face of this admitted ignorance, it is base hypocrisy for medical art to boast about conquering disease.

In fact, no doctor is competent to treat the sick until he knows more about why man is alive than medical doctors do. For he may do the body irreparable harm while thinking he is helping it.

Chiropractic

At this point it is pertinent to state that no system of treating the sick has ever grown so fast and advanced so rapidly as Chiropractic has. The reason is obvious. It recognizes Life as a Principle, not as a Product.

And no system of treating the sick has ever failed so miserably as medical art has, despite the millions of dollars wasted on it. The reason is obvious. It regards Life as a chemical Product, nor as a Cosmic Principle.

Chiropractic comes the closest to the Secret of Life by applying its primary attention to the Spinal Cord.

For the Spinal Cord carries the Life Force of the body. Hit a dog on the small of the back, and its hind legs are temporarily paralyzed.

Hit a cow back of her horns, and she falls unconscious. Cut the cord in the neck of a bull, and he drops dead quicker than if shot thru the heart.

The medical world will be amazed when we come to explain just what the Spinal Cord actually is. Even Chiropractors do not know the secret.

What Is Men?

With ancient libraries burned, ancient literature destroyed, and science in darkness, the best we can do is to consult the Bible as to the Mystery of Man.

And it tells us little. It simply says Man was made of "dust," and a Breath of Air made him a "living soul" (Gen. 2:7).

The Mystery is not that easily solved, and the Ancient Masters never wrote that statement.

But science, emerging from the Derk Ages that extended from the 5th to the 17th century, has postulated nothing better on either Life or Man.

The greet Carrel said that "we must be content with the scientific observation of our organic and mental activities; end, with no other guide, march forward into the unknown" (p.109).

But as we march, cosmic law and consistency of thought demand that we proceed in a direct manner thru infinite time to infinite results, or get lost.

Air

What element comes first in sustaining life in the body? Air.

<u>Living is breathing.</u> Even hibernating animals, sleeping all winter, must have AIR or perish. So, Air is the element that keeps Man going.

To stay the breath means to stop the life.

A soldier in Europe during World War II had his throat cut by flying steel from a bomb, and feel in a heap.

A quick examination showed no injury but a small slit out in the wind-pipe just below the larynx, causing the pipe to close so air could not enter the lungs.

A fountain pen was slipped into the windpipe to hold it open so air could enter the lungs; and the wounded man immediately rose to his feet and walked off as though nothing had happened. At a first aid station a surgeon repaired the injury, which soon healed, and the man's life was saved.

An unconscious man is devoid of all mental and intellectual powers. He knows nothing, feels nothing, sees nothing, hears nothing thinks nothing. It is as if he were dead. His body still lives, but Life ends when pressure on the medullary portion of the brain inhibits respiration.

THE MEDULLA OBLONGATA

We have seen that AIR is the element that keeps man alive, and we have found that the body's Life Center is the Medulla Oblongata, situated in the posterior and lower-most region of the skull,-- smaller than the other parts of the brain, but most important of all.

When other parts of the brain are injured, various nervous, muscular and mental functions are impaired or abolished, but Life continues. When the Medulla is damaged or destroyed, respiration ceases, and at the same moment Life in the body comes to an end.

In the face of these facts and findings, it seems ridiculous and preposterous for science to claim that Life is "The expression of a series of chemical changes."

The great Carrel called this theory "brutal materialism," and shouted: "The childish physico-chemical conceptions of man, in which physiologists and physicians believe, have to be definitely abandoned" (p.108).

Books on Anatomy divide man's brain into three sections: Cerebr --Cerebellum--and Medulla Oblongata.

The Cerebrum is the higher, frontal portion, and involved chiefly in control of voluntary motion and active external expressions of Intelligence.

The Cerebellum is the rear, lower part, and concerned with motion in various ways, and with the physical phase of Sexuality.

"Ballum" means "battle." This "battle" begins at puberty continues through Life. It is the chief theme of the Ancient Scriptures, as described by Prof. Hotema in "Son Of Perfection," and mentioned in the Bible as "War in Heaven."

The Medulla is really the upper, enlarged portion of the Spinal Cord, and, as the Life Center, is well protected by being buried under the rest of the brain. Neither can it be readily reached from below, for it rests on the base of the skull.

In the Medulla are the ganglionic nerve centers that control deglutition, vomiting, and the organs and functions of respiration.

In the process of hanging, pressure on the Medulla, not simply strangulation, is said to be the actual cause of death.

The Life Function

The Life Function is breathing, not eating. The Life Center is the Medulla, not the stomach. The Life Line is the Spinal Cord, not the intestine. The Life Element is Air not food.

The body's Life Center is a mystery to science, otherwise the claim would not be advanced that Life is "The expression of a series of chemical changes."

The reason why chiropractic has advanced so rapidly is because chiropractors are given special training on the Life Line. And even they are not taught the Life Line Secret we shall consider and discuss; for that secret is unknown to the schools.

Doctors of all schools are taught that the Spinal Cord begins in the brain as nerves, which converge at the Medulla and form the Spinal Cord. That is not only erroneous, but the doctors will be shocked when we explain the reason why.

Nerves of the Cord carry what science calls "Vital Force" to every organ, tissue and cell, making man a Living Soul. Destroy the Medulla, breathing stops, and Life ends.

O X Y G E N

What element does Air contain to give Life? Oxygen says science So, doctors put patients in oxygen tents. Still they die,--proving that Oxygen is not the complete answer.

Vital Force is an enigma to science. Science claims it is generated by the brain. Facts fail to support that claim too. When breathing stops, the Generator stops, and Life stops.

Oxygen, considered so essential to Life, forms only about 20% by volume of the Air.

Nitrogen forms about four-fifths, and science says it "acts in the atmosphere chiefly as a diluent to moderate the activity of oxygen." Whether that be true or false is not the point now.

Life Force and Vital Force appear as synonymous terms. Science says it is generated by the brain. The facts fail to support the claim.

And food energy is another false theory of science. Fill the stomach with food, but when breathing stops, living stops.

Breathing, not brain nor food, produces Vital Force, a term that tells nothing. Science cannot define it in logical terms, for it is also a myth.

All facts show that Air animates the body. No Air, No Life. That eliminates both brain and food from consideration.

And where do we go from here? Into a field so new, that what we say only a few would believe had it been said before the discovery of wireless telegraphy and radiophony.

Now it is coming to be coming knowledge in every field but Biology. Why that exception? We shall see.

Respiration

The messes know nothing as to the ridiculous theories of Respiration that prevailed from Aristotle (384-322 B.C.), down to the middle of this century.

From Aristotle to the 15th century, science believed the purpose of breathing was to "draw air into the body to cool the blood."

That silly theory gave birth to the Galenic doctrine (131-210 A.D.) that "Air introduced into the body by breathing served to regulate, to maintain, to temper, and to refrigerate the heat of the heart."

The theory as to Respiration rested there until 1643, when John Mayow discovered in the air an element he called "Spiritus Nitroserius."

Meyow said: "It may be affirmed that, in respiration, an aerial something essential to life passes into the blood (from the air). These vital particles having been extracted from the air by the blood the air expelled by the lungs is unfit to breathe again."

This important discovery by Mayow meant so little to medical art, that it lay neglected for a hundred years.

The Secret of Life lay thare bare before the eyes of the Holy Medical Hierarchy, yet it could not be seen. Perhaps it did not want to be seen.

In 1774 Priestly re-discovered Mayow's "Spiritus Nitro-sarius," and isolated a gas he termed "oxygen."

In 1782 came Lavoisier, who showed what oxygen is, thus throwing more light on the Life Function, but failing to find the Life Secret.

Then, in the middle of the 19th century; Gustav Magnus proved the presence of air gases in the blood. Now, for the first time in medical history, the function of Respiration began to assume some definite form.

But almost another century passed before medical art considered Air of sufficient importance to Life to make a special study of it.

When drugs, vaccines and serums are not involved, and the discoveries presented offer no money-making possibilities, the discoveries may be very important, but they are not attractive.

In 1924 some doctors, working at the St. Louis Infirmary in conjunction with the Washington University, concluded from their study of 1000 persons that better health and longer life for the middle aged may be achieved by "maintaining the proper level of oxygen consumption in the body."

Too Late

At last the discovery in medical circles that Air has any relation to Health and Life arrived,--but it arrived too late.

The Holy Medical Hierarchy had filled medical books with the theory that Life is "The expression of a series of chemical changes" and there the subject must rest, so far as medical art is concerned. For if medical theories are permitted to be weakened at one point, the whole system might collapse like a house of cards.

Air Dangerous

Up until the close of the 19th century, medical art considered Air so dangerous to the sick, that when the doctor arrived, he examined the patient, then ordered windows closed and fastened down, and all cracks and air-holes plugged with cotton to keep out air. He also had a heavy blanket hung around the bed so as little air as possible could reach the patient.

It took Dr. Bremer of Germany over fifty years to convince the Holy Medical Hierarchy that air is good for the sick.

But the doctors of America were determined not to let Bremer get that credit. So, they sent one of their leading lights into the New York mountains on a "fishing trip." He chanced to "discover" that fresh air is not dangerous to the sick. He even said it is good for the sick.

Another "grand, golden medical discovery." More "medical progress". Medical art is wonderful.

Millions of dollars wasted in the promotion of medical art, and it is fighting for its very life against the drugless systems that receive no outside financial support, and scent recognition from any governmental body.

Breathing

Eating and drinking are voluntary and controlled functions.

Breathing is an automatic, involuntary function, and so far beyond man's conscious control that, when asleep or unconscious from injury or other causes, he breaths better, deeper, and more rhythmically than when conscious and awake.

Breathing is the primary function of living. All other functions are secondary, and designed to keep the body fit to perform its first function.

The Lungs are perfectly designed for their work, and are by far the largest organs in the body, filling the chest from collar bone to the lowest ribs, and from spine to sternum.

The Lungs are the Organs of Life. Respiration is the Function of Life. Prof. J. S. Haldane, in his work on Respiration, wrote:

"Living is actually a struggle for air. Keep the vast lung surface supplied with fresh air, observe all other health rules, and there is no known reason, scientifically speaking, why man should ever die."

Only within the last forty years has medical art been forced to concede that fresh air is not dangerous, but actually good for the sick.

Spinal Cord.

Another mystery of the body lies before us.

Science says the Spinal Cord begins in the brain as nerves; or, the nerves of the Cord end in the brain.

If that were true, Vital Force (Nerve Force) would originate in the brain. That is what science claims.

But the brain does not generate Vital Force. Science is bewildered, and Mikkikan could not tell why he was alive.

If Life (Vital Force) originated in the brain, when brain function ceased, physical Life would end, and the Future Life would be an empty dream. That is exactly what science claims.

But Life is not a Chemical Product. It is a Cosmic Principle, and as eternal as Matter, which science concedes cannot be annihilated.

We have seen that this Cosmic Principles comes not from food, nor from the brain. So, whence its source, and what's its nature?

To hide that secret, books, scrolls, manuscripts, and libraries have been burned and men murdered.

The work of Prof. Lakhovsky titled "Secret of Life" had a hard time entering this country because it revealed the nature of Life.

The practice of book-burning to keep man in darkness has been modernized. Books are now barred from the mail for that purpose.

Why is it so important to hide the Secret of Life? If the secret were known, it would explode medical art, God would be cast down from his "throne in heaven," and the gospel Jesus could not be sold to the masses.

And furthermore, for revealing the secret which we shall disclose, we will be called everything from knave to dotard, and if we were still in the Dark Ages when the Mother Church was all powerful, we would be burnt.

The nerves of the Spinal Cord do seem to originate in the brain. They extend down the spinal canal, with countless nerves branching from the Cord and going to all parts, organs and glands of the body.

All nerves have their specific function and perform it without confusion: If some obstruction hinders the flow of nerve force at any point, the force "burns" its way thru.

Painful symptoms arise, and are given names (diagnosis) by doctors, are called "disease," and "cured" by poisons that deaden the nerves, causing them to lose much of their power, and the pain disappears. The patient is "cured."

But as the nerves recover from the shock, it causes pain to return, and the patient feels worse. Doctors cover up by calling this reaction "complications."

The patient was "cured," but unruly and unexpected "complications" arose, the patient grew worse, --and died!

"Complications" are the natural reaction of the body to the doctor's poisons called "madicine." So, the doctors kill their patients with poisons, and blame "complications." A legalized system of murder.

Part II

Union of the Astral and Physical

We now reaoh e point in man's constitution where a secret is encountered about which science and the masses know nothing.

As the nerves from ell organs and parts of the body ascend as the Spinal Cord to the brein, they pass into the Medulla and are said in medical books to end in the brain.

If that were true, whence oome Life, Mind, Consciousness, Intelligence, Vital Force, Nerve Force?

From the brain says scienoe. Where does the brain get all the mysterious qualities that constitute man? Let soience answer:

"The studies of the physiologist and physiologist ohemist abundantly indioate that all vital aotivities (of the body) are ultimately the expression of molecular rearrangements and combinations. Life, therefore, is the expression of a series of chemical changes" (Wm. Osler, greatest physiolan Amerioa aver produoed, in his Mod. Med. 1907, p. 39).

That is the materialistic law of life that binds the medical world.

And the greet Carrel got himself in bad with the Holy Medical Hierarchy when he called that "brutal materialism" (p. 317), and shouted:

"The ohildish physico-chemical conoeptions of man, in which physiologists and physicians believe, must be definitely abandoned" (p. 108).

The materialistio theory of Life rules medical art, and it is a sad failure.

Chiropraotic is rapidly advanoing because it regards Life as a Cosmic Prinoiple, not as a Chemical Produot.

Beware of the doctor who believes in "the childish physioo-chemical conceptions of man." He is dangerous.

Science thinks the nerves end in the brain beoause they seam to end. But the Sun does not rise beoause it seams to rise. Things are not what they seem.

As the nerves of the Spinal Oord enter the Medulla and spread out and penetrate different parts of the brain, they grow smaller and much finer than blood oapillaries, which were too small to be seen by the aid of the most powerful microsoope in 1616, when Dr. William Harvey shooked medical art with his disoovery of the oirouletion of the blood.

Hervey knew the blood had to pees from arteries to veins to complete the oirculation, but the oapillaries, connecting the arteries with the veins, were too tiny to be seen with his microsoope.

A similar condition of the nerves exists in the brain. There the nerves, instead of ending as science claims, grow progressively smaller, and finally, as water turns to vapor and as air changes to cellulose, they metamorphose from material fibers into bluish-white rays of astral electricity, which extend into that cosmic biological field (Astral World) which science has not yet discovered, and never will so long as it believes Life is just a Chemical Product and Vital Force is produced by the brain.

In 1954, two Canadian doctors showed by test that the leaves of beets CHANGED AIR INTO CELLULOSE IN TEN SECONDS.

The same process of metamorphose changes astral electricity into nerve fibers in the brain, and the reverse process, in the brain, changes the nerve fibers back to astral electricity.

The biblical makers destroyed so thoroughly the ancient scriptures after completing their Bible, that the only written evidence the world now has concerning the Biological Field of the Universe, appears in biblical statements so casual and unimportant as to receive little attention.

Secret of Life

We must go back and interpret some of the mysterious symbology of the Ancient Masters in order to discover the Secret of Life.

This story is related in detail by Hotema in his "Pre-Existence of Man."

It leads to the "door opened in heaven" (Rev. 4:1), and it reveals the secret of the Silver Cord and Golden Bowl mentioned in the Bible (Eccl. 12:6).

It explains the mystery of Jacob's Ladder, set up on earth, the top reaching up to heaven, with angels ascending and descending on it (Gen. 28:12).

How little do priests and preachers, and men of science and men of darkness, realize that this very ancient symbology deals with the most mysterious of all psycho-bio-physiological processes of the body, utterly unknown to endocrinologists, psychoanalysts, and biological chemists, who are all "equally ignorant of man," declared the great Carrel (p. 289).

The Silver Cord and Golden Bowl are mentioned so casually in the Bible (Eccl. 12:6), that people think they may refer to jewelry and ornaments.

Perhaps the Silver Cord was a necklace worn by the queen, and the Golden Bowl was a goblet in which servants prepared special beverages for the king.

No one would think the Silver Cord had any relationship to a creative process, or that the Golden Bowl symbolized a certain part of man.

Yet, these are what we would consider if we were properly taught that Man, not God, is the subject of the Bible, and Perfect Man, not

-34-

Jesus, is the Hero of the Bible.

And another strange statement in the Bible: "Behold! a door opened in heaven" (Rev. 4:1).

This port of entry into eternal bliss may bear some relation to the Silver Cord. The Cord may be the cable for man to scale in his ascent to his celestial home. May be the gospel Jesus used it when "he was received up into heaven, and sat on the right hand of God" (Mark 16:19).

The Silver Cord is the cosmic cable of Astral Radiation that links the Physical with the Astral. It lowers the Real Man into his terrestrial prison, where he hangs on the symbolical cross for evil purpose, with his days filled with lusts for sensation, greed, hate, jealousy, etc.

Then, when his miseries and sufferings in his physical prison are ended, the Silver Cord lifts him up to his celestial home, thru the "door opened in heaven."

So, the angels descending and ascending on Jacob's Ladder represent this journey of man; descending to the physical world in the cosmic process called Birth, and ascending to the astral world in the "born again" process called Death.

Carrel said man "can be reduced neither to a physico-chemical system nor to a spiritual entity" (p. 9).

Again, he said man is composed "of a procession of phantoms, in the midst of which there strides an Unknowable Reality" (p. 4).

These statements create confusion instead of defining man. Nor was Carrel competent to define man, hence he titled his book "Man The Unknown."

The ancient "heathens" and "savages" had a far better conception of man than can be found in the books of modern scientists. But the fragments of their writings now extant have been so badly twisted and distorted to keep man in darkness, that it is difficult to form from them a true picture of their philosophy of man.

The best that can be done is to describe man as we know him, being guided by what little we have of ancient philosophy that appears sound and logical.

The Ancient Masters considered man as constituted of four primal elements. The nature of these was concealed from the masses in the oldest and greatest of Ancient Symbols that have come down to us--the mysterious Sphinx, as explained by Hotema in his work under that title.

Extra precaution was taken by the biblical makers to conceal from the masses the correct interpretation of the Sphinx symbolism. Then, in order to deceive and mislead, they inserted wild and sensational descriptions about the "four beasts," such as those in Ezekiel (Chap. 1), Daniel (Chap. 7), and Revelation (Chap. 4, etc.), and always avoided any statement that would reveal the true nature of the beasts.

This was not accidental. It was part of a carefully planned plot to keep man in darkness as to his own nature, and to that end, books and men were burned.

If man knew himself, he would know that he has no need for gods or saviors. And the true seeker of Light will always find Light if his mind is not closed by what he has been taught in schools and colleges.

CREATION

Hermes Trismegistus, according to ancient legend, carried to Egypt from Atlantis the Ancient Masters symbology of the Zodiac and Sphinx.

The four fixed signs of the Zodiac and the symbology of the Sphinx represented the Four Creative Elements, consisting of Fire (Lion), Air (Wings, Eagle, Scorpio), Waterman (Human head), and Bull (Earth).

Fire is the Spark of Life; Air is the Breath of Life; Water is the River of Life; and Earth is the Body of Life.

These Four Principles are the foundation of all things on earth, and upon this foundation are raised the Four Bodies of Man, each composed of its own elements.

The dense body is related to the earth, the fluidal body is related to water, the mental body is related to air, and the vital body is related to fire.

The earth body is interpenetrated by the fluidal, and these two by the aerial.

Engendering, sustaining, and ruling these three is the Fire (electrical) Body, which interpenetrates all substance, causing different rates of vibration in the different densities, and making man a "living soul."

This is the ancient Riddle of the Sphinx.

Then, along comes the theologian and says, "Only God can grow a tree." What does he mean by "God"?

Observation and experience, covering a million years, prove that the Creative Elements are Soil, Solar Heat, Air and Water. These Four Principles cover the earth with everything, including the vegetal and animal kingdoms.

Now, watch the crafty work of the biblical makers as we proceed: The Four Principles were symbolized in the Sphinx, but concealed from the Masses by the "Secret Word which was in the beginning" (Jn. 1:1).

Eliphas Levi, noted French Mystic and Kaballist, described the Magic Word that "was made flesh" (Jn. 1:14). He wrote:

"The symbolical tetrad, represented in Ancient Mystery Temples by the four forms of the Sphinx, man, eagle, lion and bull, corresponded to the Four Elements of the Universe,--earth, water, air and fire.

"These four zodiacal signs, with all their analogies, explained the one Secret Word hidden in all the sanctuaries (of the ancient world)....Moreover, the Secret Word was never pronounced; it was always spelt, and expressed in four words, which were the Secret Words Yod-He-Vau-He," or Yahveh, or Je-Ho-Va, or Je-Go-Vihn, etc. (Pike, p. 763).

The Bible

This leads directly to the greatest fraud of all time. We are standing on God's doorstep, knocking on His door.

The remarkable thing about the Bible is the crafty manner in which the biblical compilers wove facts and fiction together.

There is not one chapter in it, no, not even one paragraph, where truth or falsehood is stated separately. Each falsehood is inseparably connected with an undeniable truth; and yet the true and the false are so intricately and delicately interwoven, that it is impossible for the unprepared mind to separate the one from the other.

The Bible has gone out to the world, and chained in darkness a larger number of unsuspecting people than any other secular book has ever done. And these deceived victims must live in that darkness until they shall have evolved to such mental ability that they can winnow truth from falsity and come to understand the falseness.

The Bible is the greatest book of distortion, interpolation, fraud, falsehood, and misrepresentation that man has ever produced, and the direct purpose of the work was to enthrone the church and enslave the masses.

No system of human enslavement in the history of the world has ever been so clever, cunning and complete as that termed Roman Catholicism; and its branch called Protestantism is only one short step better.

For 1600 years since Roman Catholicism was founded in the 4th century, the world has had priests, preachers, churches, seminaries, Sunday schools, sermons, lectures, conferences, synods, Bibles, Catechisms, brochures, pamphlets, retreats, monasteries, radio, TV, etc., and yet we are constrained to ask, How much have all these actually helped humanity?

During these same centuries we have had wars, hatred, slavery, poverty, drug addiction, killings, intolerance, divorces, crowded prisons, crowded insane asylums, juvenile delinquency. Something must be wrong.

Biblical Distortion

The first verses of the John present an excellent example of the crafty manner in which the biblical makers wove facts and fiction together.

We have shown what the "Word" actually means. The John begins, "In the beginning was the Word, and the Word was with God, and the Word was God."

Then the ancient scriptures were destroyed so the masses would know nothing about the real meaning of the "Word" that was "God."

The "Word" was made flesh,--is true, as we have seen. The "Word" represented the Four Creative Elements of which man's body is composed.

To hide these facts, the ancient scriptures had to be destroyed after the Bible had been copied from them.

Now, the ancient facts are revealed, and none can be offended whose mind is open and who is looking for Light and Truth.

Solar Man

The Spark of Life, the Fire Body, the Solar Body, the Eternal Body, has neither beginning of days, nor end of life (Heb. 7:1-3).

It is amazing to observe how the Fire Body engenders and interpenetrates the other bodies of man.

We would be astonished if we could see in its entirety the Nerve System, in which the Solar Man lives and works. For it would present to the eye the same size, shape and form of our dense body.

The nerves are the Fire Body; and the point of a pin cannot be pressed against the body anywhere without touching a nerve. When we gaze in a mirror we little suspect that we are actually looking at Solar Man.

Science calls nerve force "food energy" or "chemical action," or "a series of chemical changes." Greater ignorance cannot be found anywhere.

The great Carrel said; "In fact, our ignorance (of man) is profound." "It is impossible, for the present, to grasp (the body's) constitution. We must, then, be content with the scientific observation of our organic and mental activities, and, without any other guide, march forward into the unknown" (p. 109).

That statement of a great scientist sounds very different from the hogwash and hokum contained in the controlled press and censored periodicals. But let any medical doctor attack that hogwash and hokum, and he is quickly called up on the carpet, his licensed revoked for "unethical conduct," and he is smeared and disgraced as an enemy to humanity.

Life and Vital Force

Life, vital force, nerve force, call it what you will, is solar or astral electricity.

The Real Man is the Fire Man, the Solar Man, the Electrical Man. Crile, Osborn, Secor, Gilbert, Gray, and scores of other scientists, declared that even the cells of the body are electrical machines.

Whence comes the electricity? The air is saturated with it. But the Sun is the source of the electricity which covers the earth with every living thing on it. Solar Worship is the oldest of all religions.

Osborn asserted that "Our distinctive characteristics and functions are the properties of the Sun." From where else could they come?

Secor said the functions of the body "Are the result of solar radiation, ruled by intelligence inherent in the body cells," and in the atoms and electrons. For atoms and electrons could not perform definite processes without the intelligence to do it.

But as late as 1940, a well-known British medical doctor declared: "We hardly know anything about the effects of cosmic radiation on human beings."

And right here before us is the Solar Fire, in the form of Cosmic Radiation, that makes man a "living soul."

The true words are A LIVING SUN.

So complete is the ignorance and confusion of science as to Biology, that the great Millikan admitted, "I cannot explain why I am alive."

The Fire Body is Solar Man,--the Melchisedek of the Bible, having neither beginning of days, nor end of life (Heb. 7:1-3).

But no one tell the man of darkness that he is the Melchisedek of that allegory.

Consciousness--Mind--Intelligence

What can science tell us about Consciousness, Mind and Intelligence? Nothing.

Who can separate these qualities and show where the one begins and the other ends? No one.

Authors write about Cosmic Consciousness, and in their attempt to explain what they mean, they get lost in their own words.

Sir William Crookes, one of the world's greatest scientists, said in 1895, that the Atom possesses the Consciousness, Mind and Intelligence to choose its own path, to reject and to select, and has the qualities of sensation and volition.

The four properties of the Atom, attraction, repulsion, sensation and volition, form what the Ancient Masters termed the Cross of Life, as explained by Hotema in "Pre-Existence of Man."

Transformative processes present these four fundamental functions of Life, inherent in the Atom and exhibited by the cells of man's body.

These four properties of the Atom are responsible for the production of everything on earth, called Nature, of which man is a part.

Without these four fundamental properties of the Atom, there
would be no creation, no transformation, no organized forms, no Life,
no Universe, and no God.

Atoms possess the power to do work, forming everything in the
Universe. This proves they possess Consciousness of what they are
doing, Mind to guide them in their work, and Intelligence to have
their processes produce definite ends.

Atomic Consciousness is Cosmic Consciousness not only, but also
Cosmic Mind and Cosmic Intelligence.

The Atom is a living entity, a vibrant world, and man's body is
nothing but a mass of atoms. The facts are evident and the conclusions are definite.

All the powers and qualities that religion attributes to its God
are in the Atom.

Part III

Cosmic Radiation

Cosmic Radiation is now a common term. Yet, it has been only
a quarter of a century since Sir James Jeans first drew attention to
its effect on man.

And as late as 1940, medical art admitted that it had nothing
concerning the effect of cosmic radiation on humanity. In fact, it
has nothing now.

And Cosmic Radiation leads directly into the field of Astrology,
the greatest of all sciences, and the most bitterly condemned of
all.

Now, this condemned science of the Ancient Masters is being re-
discovered; and it leads into the realm of Atomism, the craze of the
day and a field so startling that the whole world is thrilled,--
thrilled by the re-discovery of an ancient science that was develope
and perfected by the "star-mongers", who have been called everything
but intelligent men.

Astrology treated of the powers of Sun and Stars, and their
effects upon everything on earth, including the vegetal and animal
kingdoms.

Millikan, who could not explain why he was alive, said:

"Cosmic radiation penetrates practically a thousand feet into
the earth's crust --- Cosmic rays must contact the earth's magnetic
field (eura) as electrons of more than 10 million volts" (Cosmic
Radiation, Colston Papers, 1949).

The resistance of the earth's aure to cosmic radiation is said
to equal that of approximately six feet of lead.

Earth's Aura

The earth's aura forms an electro-magnetic field, surrounding
the earth and extending approximately 4500 miles thru to outerspace.

When cosmic radiation strikes the centripetal and centrifugal
forces of the earth's aura, one effect is the creation of an Atmospheric Soil called the Astral Plane by the Ancient Masters, which
was described in their astrological system, and said to contain the
VIRILITY OF ALL LIFE.

Of the Atmospheric Soil, Anaximenes (380-320 B.C.), said:

"The Essence of the Universe is in the Infinite Air in eternal
movement, which contains ALL IN ITSELF. Everything is formed by in-
tegration and disintegration of the AIR under the Law of Expansion
and Contraction."

In the discovery of wireless telegraphy and radiophony, science
has re-discovered the Astral World of the Ancient Masters, commonly
celled heaven, which contains the essence or germ of all that appears
on earth, called Nature, and without which the earth would be as

barren as a stone.

We shall observe how the biblical makers excluded what the Masters wrote on the Astral World, in order to keep man in darkness as to himself and his eternal home, except some minor statements that tell nothing of this secret of Creation.

For instance, in the Bible it is said that every plant of the field (was in the astral world) before it was in the earth, and every herb of the field (was in the astral world) before it grew (in the earth) (Gen. 2:5).

Immutalbe law and consistency of thought demand that we include in this pre-existence in the Astral World, all animals and man as being in the Astral World as an Archetypal Entity before appearing on earth in physical form.

In fact, the man on the earth plane is only a suspension of the Archetypal Entity of the Astral World.

The World of Life.

The Atmospheric Soil is the Biological Field of the Universe, the Astral Plane of the Ancient Masters, the Heaven of the theologian, but not the Heaven that the preacher pictures in his sermon nor to himself.

From the Astral World emenates the Astral Beam that unites the physical and astral planes, and covers the earth with all living things, called Nature.

When the body's Fiery Rays (Nerves) enter the brain from the Spinal Cord, they do not end, as science says. They CHANGE from physical fibers to Astray Rays, passing out of the head, thru the Frontioulus Frontalis, as an X-Ray Beam, into the Atmospheric Soil.

This fontanel is the soft spot in the top of a baby's head, where the skull closes not immediately. Sometimes it never closes, but usually the sutures unite between the second and fifth years.

Unto this day the monks of all nations shave their hair over this spot, to give unobstructed passage to the Silver Cord thru the "door opened in heaven."

The ancient scrolls of India, beyond the destructive hand of the biblical makers, termed the Fontioulus Frontalis the Barhmarandhra, the Aperture of Brahma, the Throne of Siva, the Seat of the Nibodhika Fire.

The biblical makers knew the secret of the Astral Plane and the Silver Cord, but they destroyed the musty scrolls and distorted what they copied, to hide the secret and keep man in darkness.

The Ego

The Cosmic Unit (Ego), constituted of Four Seed Atoms, is conveyed by the Silver Cord down thru the "door opened in heaven," called the Gateway of the Soul, and appears on earth as Man, greatest of all mysteries, causing Carrel to declare:

"Man is made up of a procession of phantoms, in the midst of which there strides an Unknowable Reality" (Man The Unknown, p. 4). The "Unknowable Reality" is the Ego.

Penetrating the skull as an X-Ray Beam at the Fonticulue Frontalis, the Silver Cord enters the brain as an invisible beam, gradually growing visible as nerves, and converging at the Medulla, there forming the Spinal Cord as Hotema explains in "Pre-Existence of Man.

Thru the nerves, the brain controls the body. The brain, in turn, is governed by the Astral Plane thru the Silver Cord by Cosmic Consciousness, as Hotema explains in more detail in "Son of Perfection."

This grand Secret of Life was so carefully concealed by the biblical makers, that the Silver Cord is mentioned but once in the Bible and then in terms that tell nothing to the unitiated.

The Silver Cord may appropriately be compared to the umbilical cord that links the embryo to the mother.

It is the Actral Beam of Solar Electricity that links terrestrial man to celestial man, referred to by Paul as the spiritual body, ... "eternal in the heavens" (1 Cor. 15:55; 2 Cor. 5:1).

The Silver Cord links the Microcosm to the Macrocosm, the Progeny to the Progenitor, the Product to the Producer.

Man's body is a mass of millions of suns and stars, organized into systems of cells, molecules, atoms and electrons, all revolving at terrific speed.

It is preposterous to hold that this propelling power comes from food, or from the "expression of a series of chemical changes."

The power emanates from the Astral World and consists of Cosmic Radiation.

Radio Beam

We can form a good conception of the Silver Cord by thinking of a Radio Beam that extends miles into the other, along which airships may be guided accurately and safely.

Man can make and direct pilotless planes and control his missiles by radio and radar, but little suspects that he is copying a Creative Process by which he is produced, preserved, directed and controlled by an astral ray called the Silver Cord.

Some interesting observations on the Silver Cord were made by Dr. Arthur A. Beale, who wrote:

"There have been cases, even to our own knowledge, where patient have left their bodies and were able to look down from above on their unconscious shell.

"In such instances the complete entity (ego, mind, consciousness intelligence) is out of the body, and yet remains anchored to it by a tenuous Cord of astral substance, by means of which the entity may return to and activate the shell again, provided the cord is not broken. ...

"If a trained occultist, or even a true clairvoyant, were present at the time, he could see and describe the comotose body and the divorced or separated entity hovering over it, joined by the (silver) cord." -- Evolution of Mind, p. 45).

Radar Beams

Gradually we are progressing back to the point where we can somewhat understand the fiction, fable, parable and symbol of ancient scriptures.

The press of June 1, 1957, carried a news item, stating that invisible Radar Beams can be fatal to humans.

Two doctors working on radar development during World War II, discovered that in less than a minute invisible Radar Beams can kill a man.

In 10 seconds a technician in an electronics plant in Los Angeles, standing in the beam of a radar transmitter, felt sensations of heat in his abdomen. In less than a minute the intensity of the heat made him move out of the range of the invisible rays.

Within two weeks the man died. The surface of his body showed no marks -- "but his insides were cooked," said the doctors. "A hole as big as a silver dollar was burned in his small bowel."

Dr. John T. McLaughlin, one of the doctors, said that microwaves emitted by a radar transmitter can penetrate the walls of a building and cause instant, intolerable heat in man's body.

The invisible Radar Ray may be the destructive phase of the Silver Cord under the blind direction of man. Or it may be the Silver Cord in reverse. Under certain conditions the rays of the sun are constructive, while they are destructive under other conditions.

Disease

The surface of man's body shows no signs of the action of the Silver Cord, and its force in health cannot be felt.

But things go wrong quickly when any obstruction hinders its natural flow. Then pains appear, -- a condition doctors call "disease," the profitable bogey of medical art.

This "disease" doctors attempt to "cure" with virulent poisons, -- poisons no doctor would ever think of giving to the well.

This stupid, absurd, unnatural practice is the direct cause of the dangerous "complications" which kill so many victims of medical doctors.

The first effect of the doctor's poisons is deceptive. They dull the nerves, weaken vital action, and produce a state of bodily quiescence that deceives the doctor, causing him to think his poisons have helped the patient.

Then comes the natural reaction, the secondary effect, a logical state that follows as the nerves begin to revive and recover from the shock as the paralyzing effect of the poisons (medicine) begins to wear off.

This reaction is what the doctors call "complications." The more vital the patient, the more intense the reaction, and the more serious the "complications."

This reaction is often so violent in the case of vital patients as the nerve system recovers from the shock of the poisons, that the strongest poisons of medical art are unable to subdue the "symptoms of the disease," as they are called.

Now the doctor is "at the end of his rope." "Medical science" has done its best,--and lost the battle against "disease."

All the doctor can do now, is to use his strongest poisons to subdue the patient's vitality in his efforts to give the suffering victim some relief.

The poisons finally overcome the vitality of the nerve system, and the well-poisoned victim sinks into a peaceful coma,--out of which he usually fails to revive.

The end is near. It generally comes quickly. Friends and relatives stand by and witness the victim's "death struggle."

This deadly system of legalized murder has been killing people for hundreds of years; and it will continue its deadly work until the outraged masses rise up in their might, and demand legal protection against such an antiquated, unscientific, unnatural, preposterous, dangerous, murderous system.

Born Again

In "Pre-Existence of Man," Hotema says that during the dying process, man can see his body as he leaves it, but not clearly, due to a dim haze between him and his body.

This haze is the Silver Cord which contains the Ego, the Real Man, and thru it he looks as one looks thru a veil over one's face.

Like a radio beam, the Silver Cord is capable of practically infinite extension. In sleep, we may, as in dreams, leave the body thru the "door opened in heaven" end fly miles away, yet the body still lives and we return to it,--provided the Silver Cord remains intact. When the Cord breaks, death of the body ensues immediately.

Death would never frighten any one if the facts were known. It is as natural to die as to be born. It is as painless as eating and as natural as breathing. And the cosmic powers that provide for our coming also provide for our going.

What actually happens in the death process is just a CHANGE of Consciousness, from its focal point in the earth body to the focal point in the Solar Body.

The Bible calls this "change" a mystery (1 Cor. 15:51).

Take the "mystery" out of religion and religion would vanish. It would be replaced with a Philosophy of Life, such as that of the Ancient Masters, which was destroyed when the Roman Catholic Church was born in the 4th century.

The process of leaving the body in death is described by one who recovered from a death-like swoon, as like struggling thru a dark, narrow tunnel out into a big, brightly lighted place.

How similar to being born in the flesh. The typical experience of the infant during and immediately after being born of the mother.

In the cosmic process of dying, the Mind grows clearer than ever before; and the head becomes intensely brilliant, like a Golden Bowl (Eccl. 12:6).

The Silver Cord also grows stronger, to protect the Ego; and "the etheric body," says one author, "flows out (of the Fonticulus Frontalis) thru the Silver Cord like a rapidly moving fluorescent light, imperceptibly extracting the body's vitality, somewhat as a suction, and the Ego leaves the body thru the top of the head as an etheric light that may be seen by a true clairvoyant (Cosmic Fire, p. 86).

That describes the dreaded, terrifying, physiological process of dying, the "born again" mystery, which is all over, says the Bible, "in the twinkling of an eye" (1 Cor. 15:52).

The Seed Atoms

The Cosmic Unit, originating in the Astral World, is said to be composed of Four Seed Atoms, corresponding to the Four Principles, each having its own Seed Atom.

This is the Real Man that leaves the body in death thru the "door opened in heaven," and appears as an electric spark which can be seen by the true clairvoyant.

During the Dark Ages some were so unwise as to say they could see the Light leaving the body, and were burned as "witches." Even now those who can see that Light had better keep silent.

The Ego is constituted of Four Seed Atoms so small, that almost a million would form a speck scarcely visible under the most powerful microscope.

The experiences of man during his earthly life are impressed upon the Ego as a message on a phonograph record. That is the reason why it is possible for the hypnotist to have his subject describe events that occurred during antecedent incarnations, as in the Bridey Murphy case, which also provides further proof of the Doctrine of Reincarnation.

While the other atoms of the dense body are renewed from time to time, the Seed Atoms (Ego) remain fixed and permanent, from one incarnation to the next.

The real creator of man is the Cosmic Unit of Four Seed Atoms, not an imaginary god.

The Cosmic Unit leaves the body at death, but returns to the earth at the dawn of another physical life, to serve as the nucleus around which is built the dense body to be used on earth by the same Ego. The time between incarnations may be 500 years, 1000 years or 10,000 years.

The Doctrine of Reincarnation was taught by the Ancient Masters who claimed they had evidence to prove the truth of it. The biblica makers at Alexandria were careful to exclude that phase of ancient philosophy.

When the Ego prepares to leave the dense body, the Silver Cord remains intact until the panorama of one's past life has been etched into the Seed Atoms.

Life After Death

Of course there is no such thing as death. It is a process of re-birth, and would be understood if the facts were not suppressed by the church.

Much literature exists on the subject of survival after what we call death.

If we survive after the death of the body, then we exist before being born in the flesh. For something cannot come from nothing.

In that very ancient work called "Book of The Dead," claimed to have been written by the Egyptian Thoth (Hermes), it is said that Osiris, the Egyptian god, had the power to be born again, and to look down on his body at death. That applies to all men.

On the wall of the ancient Egyptian temple of Denders appeared the Zodiac, with a group of scenes depicting the death and resurrection of Osiris, who said: "I am the resurrection and the life." --Budge, vol. 22, pp. 126,141,312.

Be not misled by the word "resurrection." It does not mean the resurrection of a dead physical body, but the departure of the Ego from the dying body.

In his "Pre-Existence of Man", Hotema cites a case where the Ego left the body during a surgical operation, then returned to the body and, when the body recovered consciousness, related the details of gazing down at the body during the operation.

Leaving the Body

As the Silver Cord breaks, the Real Man is released from his earthly prison, and that is a moment of great importance to the Ego.

It cannot be too strongly urged upon the relatives of a dying person that it is a crime against the departing Ego to give expressions to loud lamentations.

At that moment the Ego is engaged in a process of supreme importance, and much of the value of the past life depends upon the attention the Ego can give to the matter at this time. Loud lamentations of those present seriously disturb that attention.

Also, it is a crime against the dying person to use stimulants to force the departing Ego back into the body, thus giving a great shock to a dying person.

It is peaceful to leave the body, but torturous to be forced back into it by stimulants, to endure more suffering in the body.

Relatives think they are aiding a dying person by trying to keep him alive. That is a mistake. In that way many are kept dying for hours, thus prolonging the suffering in the body.

Fontanels

There are seven areas between the skull bones called fontanels, the largest being the Fontioulus Frontalis, easily felt in the top of a new-born baby's head. It remains open for a considerable time after birth, and exhibits a rhythmical pulsation,--a point to be remembered. For right here lies the secret of all the pulsation of the body.

In the formation of the body, the brain develops first, and is really a materialization of the Silver Cord. That area of the skull where this primary work occurs is the Fontioulus Frontalis. But to this fontanel science pays no especial attention. If it has any particular purpose science knows nothing about it.

And unknown to science, the Silver Cord and Spinal Cord are actually a continuation of each other. The Spinal Cord is the material extension of the Silver Cord.

At the lower end of the Spinal Cord in the body, is the creative power of the Microcosm; and at the upper end of the Silver Cord, in the Astral World, is the Cosmic Creative Power of the Macrocosm,-- the power that the church falsely attributes to its imaginary God.

This secret of the body's constitution, unknown to science, was jealously guarded by the Masters; and the biblical makers were most careful to exclude all traces of it from their Bible.

And so, the plunging of man in darkness, and the invention and promotion of the church God and his son Jesus, made the church great rich and powerful.

But the church has had to wage war constantly against the Light of Knowledge to keep from being sunk; and in spite of its bitter fight against the Truth that sets men free, the tide is turning and the final fall is only a question of time.

The press reported that church attendance for 1956 fell two million below that of 1955, and we know of the great decline suffered by the church in Russia.

But which is the worst--Christian Fraud or Communist Enslavement

Universal Rhythm

The function of the cells, organs, glands, brain and nerve system is not the result of "chemical changes" occurring in the body. nor the beating of the heart, nor the flowing of the blood.

These are the Life Functions, about which science knows almost nothing.

Astral Radiation, flowing as the Silver Cord from the Astral World, is Nerve Force, Vital Force, Life Force. It could be called Cosmic Vibration, and is the cause of the beating of the heart, the flowing of the blood, and all pulsation of the body, glands, organs and cells.

Astral Radiation does not originate in the body, but in the Astral World.

Scientists wonder as they observe the rhythm of cosmic force, but fail to see that rhythm in all body functions. They are the expressions of Universal Rhythm, exhibited by Stars and Suns, and flowing into the body as the Silver Cord.

Scientific works are silent on this subject, describing nothing definite, but erroneously asserting that heart action and vital action are the result of "nerve force."

What "nerve force" is, science does not know.

So, we must go way back to the Lost Wisdom of the ancient "heathens" and "savages" to learn what we have, that tells us anything about the Mystery of Man and the Secret of Life which harmonized with known facts.

Science can have nothing to offer for human betterment until it leads to a solution of the Mystery of Life.

Take the "mystery" out of life and that will end the Darkness of Religion and the Fraud of medicine.

Light will come with the discovery of the Secret of Life. And that discovery will ruin the twin frauds, Medical Art and Christianity. Their leaders know it only too well, and that is the reason why L I F E remains in the realm of darkness and mystery.

(The End)

CHIROPRACTIC THE GREATEST

By Prof. Hilton Hotema.

Part I.

In 1895, Dr. Daniel David Palmer discovered a new, drugless method of treating the sick. It was given the name of Chiropractic, a Greek term, meaning "done with the hands."

The exact nature of the discovery was unknown to Palmer, and still remains unknown to the profession unto this day.

It deals with the body's Nerve System. Nerves are charged with force so mysterious in its nature, that science has been unable to analyze it. Doctors call it "nerve Force" because it operates thru the nerves. The name does not define the force nor describe its origin.

Dr. Willard Carver, a tall, Iowa lawyer, saw something in Chiropractic and became associated with Palmer, looking after the legal aspect of the new discovery. In 1906, he founded the Carver Chiropractic College at Oklahoma City, and wrote the text-books it uses.

In referring to the force that animates the "Zygote" in the female uterus, Carver refused to discuss its nature or its source. He wrote:

"The temptation to enter the realm of speculation as to what is the 'new vitality' which manifests itself at this time (in the zygote will be repressed, for it has not yet been given man to know" (Psycho Bio-Physiology, pp. 194-5).

The "new vitality" vitalizing the zygote seems to come from nowhere, and promptly assumes with full authority the task of building a new person,--the great mystery of existence.

No eye can see the "new vitality." No science in modern times has defined it. What is it? "Life," says the doctor.

What is Life? What is its nature? and whence its source? To these embarrassing questions all the great doctors are very silent.

DARKNESS

Carefully concealed from the eyes of the world is the fact that medical art is in deep darkness as to the nature of Life. The public is not told the haughty physicians admit that they cannot explain why they are alive.

That admission of ignorance on a point so vital is sufficient to bar all medical doctors from the sick-room. For it is definitely dangerous for doctors to treat the sick when they know not why the body functions.

Think of a mechanic tampering with a sick automobile and knowing nothing of the nature of its motivative power, or believing the power is generated by the motion of the machine, as doctors believe in the case of the body.

The doctors think the body functions because it functions. A man runs because he runs. The reason why doctors do not kill more of their patients is because the body can take so much and still live.

Unknown to the masses is the fact that to blot out all knowledge of the nature of Life, millions of dollars have been spent, libraries burnt, and ancient temples and cities destroyed.

That secret was discovered ages ago by the Astrologers, and the processes of Life, in the development of man, they portrayed in the marvellous symbology of the Zodiakos. And yet, to discredit these great scientists and to condemn their brilliant work, they have been called everything from knaves to dotards to make the world sneer their memory and see them as "superstitious heathens."

Why were millions spent and great destruction wrought to conceal the nature of Life? For the very good reason that knowledge of the nature of Life would remove all fear of death, and ruin the greatest money-making schemes on earth.

Accordingly, no price was too great to pay in order to keep the masses in darkness so the church could sell its god and its Jesus to the multitude.

Re-discovered

After fifty years of diligent research, Prof. Hotema has dug from ancient ruins some fragments of ancient scriptures dealing with a marvellous secret of the Macrocosm, and tells the story in his remarkable work "The Flame Divine" (The Breath of Life and the Flame Divine is the final title).

He shows why Chiropractic is the greatest system known for treatment of the sick. It lies in the fact that Chiropractic unconsciously deals with the Fire of Life, and has some knowledge as to why the body functions. And yet, it knows not the true nature of the animative power nor the seat of its source.

Hotema shows that the secret was solved by the Ancient Astrologers and lies buried now beneath the ruins of their temples, libraries and cities. Such of their valuable scriptures as were salvaged are concealed in caves in India and are guarded by armed men.

The old Masters discovered a scientific principle of immense sweep and simplicity, and called it Astral Light. Modern science calls it Cosmic Radiation.

The Ancient Astrologers found that as Astral Light contacts the earth's aura, it creates an Aeriferous Substance which they termed the Atmospheric Soil that contains the Virility of all Life.

Some scraps of this ancient wisdom have accidentally filtered down to us thru the writings of Anaximenes (380-320 B.C.) who declared, "The Essence of the Universe is in the Infinite Air in eternal motion which contains ALL in itself."

Then he showed that the Visible World develops from Air. When exceedingly attenuated, Air becomes fire; when more condensed, wind; a still further condensation produces clouds; greater compression changes clouds to water; further pressure produces the earth; and finally, rock is formed as matter becomes still more condensed; these successive changes being produced by temperature changes and by motion which is constant and eternal.

He termed the Aeriferous Substance surrounding the earth an Animative Essence, in continuous motion, constantly changing its form and generating new things,--things not contained, as such, in the primitive homogenous substance.

Then he declared that Cosmic Motivative Power is Fire. We know by experience that Fire makes the steam-engine move, the gas-engine move, the automobile move. That lightning and electricity are Fire. And, according to the Bible, the God of the Jews was Fire (Deut. 4:24 9:3; Ps. 50:3; Heb. 12:29, etc.).

Ancient Science held that Fire is exceedingly attenuated Air. Heraclitus (535-475 B.C.) considered all things derived from Fire, and eventually transformed again to Fire.

The Pythagoreans regarded Fire as the Heart of the Universe, the Monad or First Form. Fire extended from the earth to the limits of the Cosmos. All things were derived from Fire, and strive ever to return to Fire.

Part II

Chiropractic The Greatest

The Flame Divine

"I sense One Flame, O Gurudeva; I see countless undetached spark shining in it" (Secret Doctrine, Blavatsky).

The Spark of Life is a term often used, and its meaning is much more literal than poetical.

The Great Pyramid of Gizeh, an ancient temple of Initiation, symbolized the Terrestrial Flame, rising to unite with its Celestial Counterpart.

So the Neophyte, in his initiation, was taught the secret of the Philosophy of Fire and shown that he was the Terrestrial Flame Divine.

Pain in the physical body is a sensation of the Celestial Fire, as it strives to remove some obstruction in its path. Never kill the pain with poison, but remove the obstruction and the pain will vanish.

The first religion of which we have any accurate account was that of Atlantis; and this religion was the Philosophy of Fire. It showed that the real man is the Flame Divine.

Man would be amazed could he see his Nerve System in its entirety. For it would present to the eye the same size, shape and form of his physical body.

A pin point cannot be pressed against the body anywhere without touching a nerve. That is the Astral Body, the Man of Fire, the Flame Divine.

At this point we come face to face with the most amazing secret of the Constitution of Man.

Medical books say nerves begin in the brain and end in various parts and organs of the body. Were that true, then Vitality, Conscio ness, Mind and Intelligence would not only be the greatest of all miracles, but their nature would defy description. And that is exact ly where medical art is at this hour.

These four mysterious qualities combined constitute what we call Life, and, according to medical art, they spring from nothingness. Or perhaps they rise from internal chemical action. It's all a profound mystery to the medical world.

Science correctly holds that, under cosmic law, the greater cannot come from the lesser. But in the case of man, medical art recognizes no law. Everything about his body results from accident and chance. Even his ailments.

Nerves seem to begin in the brain, but do not. The sun seems to rise, but does not. The earth seems motionless, but is not. Our senses deceive us. And yet medical doctors depend entirely on obsarvation as to man's ailments.

When Harvey shocked medical art in 1616 with the announcement of his discovery of the circulation of the blood, haughty physicians just sneered. He could not explain how the blood passes from arteries to veins. No connecting tubes could be seen by the aid of the best microscopes then available.

Harvey knew the blood must flow from arteries to veins to complete the circuit; but he could not explain the mystery. Arteries seemed to end in nothing, and veins seemed to begin in nothing. So, nerves in the brain seem to begin from nothing.

Materialization

Ancient Science knew the nerves could not begin in the brain from nothing. For they are charged with power that does not originate in the brain.

The power comes from an external source, and there had to be some connection between the nerves and the source. Harvey knew there had to be some connection between arteries and veins.

Now, let the haughty physicians sneer again: Cranial nerves seem to begin in the brain from nothing, but do not. This is the point where Microcosm and Macrocosm unite. Evidence of the unition is the Astral Force in the Nerve System.

As ice is materialized vapor; and as sun-rays materialize to form the colors of the rainbow, so Astral Rays materialize to form the Nerve System.

As Astral Rays penetrate the brain, they transform into nerve fibers by the process of materialization.

The transition of Radiation to Matter and Matter to Radiation is now an established fact.

Atoms are transformed into radiation, as in radioactivity, and radiation into Matter, as photons of gamma rays.

This discovery established the fact that "creation" is a process of condensation of Astral Radiation, and its transformation into physical forms according to the intelligence and law that inhere in Astral Radiation.

This new understanding of Radiation and Matter is the great miracle of the ages. By this pattern we understand the astral origin of visible forms, including man.

Intelligence is not confined to the brain. It appears in the vegetal kingdom, and in cosmic elements, which rigidly obey the law, —far more than those usually do who possess brains.

And that solves the Secret of Life,—well understood by Ancient Science but a profound mystery to the medical world.

This knowledge is concealed from the eyes of the world in biblical symbols and allegories. Now follow us and see for yourself:

Astral Rays extend from the Aeriferous Substance, converge as the Silver Cord says ancient literature (Eool. 12:6), at the Fonti-oulus Frontalis, termed in ancient scripture "door opened in heaven" (Rev. 4:1), in the top of the skull, called "Golden Bowl" in the Bible (Eool. 12:6), and there transform from invisible rays to material fibers,--the visible beginning of the Nerve System, and the great mystery of man's constitution.

In fact, the brain, like the nerves, is condensed Rays; and so far independent of food are brain and nerves, that man may die of starvation and the brain and nerves remain unimpaired.

Part III.

Chiropractic The Greatest

Power of Astral Rays

Nerves are analogous to electric wires, and carry force that is a mystery to science. The force is astro-electricity. It flows to all organs and parts of the body, producing that state of activity called Life. So, Life is the effect of Astral Radiation acting on the body thru the nerves.

Besides the visible nerve system, there is an invisible astral system, described in ancient "Tantric Literature" as nadistic; but the limited space at our disposal here prevents our expatiating thereon.

The search for a Life Principle will always end in failure; for Life is not an entity but a name applied to the effects of Astral Radiation manifesting in a material form which is built by the force that operates and controls it.

With cessation of the force, bodily function ends,--and that, says Evolutionism, is the end of man. But, said Ancient Science, the body is not man. It is only the vehicle used by man on the terrestrial plane.

Chiropractic Success.

No system of treating the sick has ever grown so fast, against strong medical opposition, as Chiropractic has. The reason is obvious: It recognizes Life as a power distinct from the body.

No system of treating the sick has ever failed so miserably as medical art has, despite billions of dollars wasted on it. The reason is obvious: It regards Life as nothing more than a physico-chemical product, generated in the body.

Chiropractic is a scientific system of treating the ailing body which is so remarkable that as yet its great value has not been appreciated.

And Chiropractic applies to the entire body, and at all times. It does not apply to one ailment or a few ailments, but to all ailments.

Its progress would be so great as to startle the world if it were free from powerful medical opposition, and had for research and advertising the millions of dollars that are wasted on that unscientific system of experimentation called medical art.

Chiropractic succeeds because it deals with the Nerve System, the Astral Body, the Flame Divine.

Medical art fails because it deals with tricky, unreliable, changeable symptoms, and changes treatment as symptoms change. A hit-or-miss method, based on observation, speculation, conjecture, etc. It has no law nor principles.

Chiropractic research shows that no doctor can make a drop of blood, consequently, no doctor can make anything that will help the body. The very best the best doctor can do is to see that nothing is done to the sick body to damage it.

The body can make no use of medicines, remedies, drugs, vaccines, serums, and all the other poisons used by medical art. These poisons cripple and kill many, but cure none.

The body manufactures its own products and can use no other. This law of the living body is in force at all times in good health and bad health, and is never nullified nor modified by its ailments. The body in all conditions remains always subject to the same immutable law.

Medical art uses many schemes to crush Chiropractic because of its grand success. Chiropractors are arrested on false charges of "Practicing medicine without a license," when the real reason is that of getting the sick well after the sufferers were abandoned as incurable by medical doctors.

The sordid attitude of medical art clearly shows that the sick are supposed to DIE FOR THE GLORY OF MEDICINE if they do not respond to regular medical treatment.

Medical art is one of the biggest frauds on earth. Its history is a tale of fatal errors, and its path is strewn with the bones of its trustful victims. It kills and cripples many but cures none. It is nothing more than the voodooism of the savage modernized by chicanery, animated by trickery, and perpetuated by sophistry. It should be outlawed as a positive menace to mankind.

(The   End)

NOTE: We have no authority to comment on the works of Prof. Hotema. Our
e   lish and sell the works   obli ation ends.
And we have no authority to give anyone is   are written to
be accepted or   cted and to cause the re er o   . Many who rejected
certain titles years ago, will find that the same books are accepted by
them now.

(This page has been re-typed from the original copy, which stencil was torn, therefore the difference in type style. However, the entire copy is here, exactly as in the original).

Our work titled SON OF PERFECTION, which will show how Chapter 2 of Genesis is linked with Revelation, and that Perfect Man is he who has obeyed the command not to eat of the forbidden fruit, has overcome his desires and mastered himself. The ancient Masters considered the man who conquered himself as greater than he who conquered a city.

The Apocalypse

Strangest book of the Bible.
Oldest book of the Bible.
Last book of the Bible.

A book so strange that the best brains of the Christian clergy have never been able to interpret it.

A book so old that its origin is lost in the night of time.

A book so baffling that the church refused to consider it or to allow it to become a part of the Bible until the 18th century; and then it was embraced with open arms--for a most peculiar reason.

What explanation can the church offer for the reason why the gospel Jesus was made the hero of a book that was written by the Ancient Masters of India thousands of years before the world ever heard of him?

That burning question has a strange answer, and it shall be given in this work to an amazed Christian world.

In the oldest Greek scro l the title of this book was simply "Apocalypse," a Greek word meaning to reveal, to disclose, to disrobe, to unveil, and that was the reason why the church translated the title "Revelation,"--yet to the clergy it reveals nothing; and Isis wrapped in her peplum was never more safe from the eyes of the world than is the inner meaning of the Apocalypse.

Primarily, the Apocalypse has no relation to theology, to heaven, or to God, in its true interpretation, as we shall show in this work. And it has no more reason to be included in the Bible than has the Ritual of the Freemasons.

For the Apocalypse is an attempt to describe, in symbol and allegory, the sensations and emotions which are experienced by the neophyte as he goes thru the various phases of the solemn ceremony of initiation in the Ancient Mysteries, as we have explained in our work titled Mysterious Sphinx, pp. 27-30.

It would be similar to an attempt to describe the sensations ar emotions of a candidate who went thru the various phases of the cermony of initiation in the Masonic Lodge.

That is exactly what the Apocalypse is. It is a description, symbol and allegory, of the sensations and emotions experienced by the neophyte as his body and mind reacted and responded to the strang things he encountered in the various tests applied to him as he went thru the trials of initiation.

And these psychic emotions and physical sensations are describe in terms of cosmic phenomena, as the glare of lightning, the roll of thunder, the shock of the earthquake, and the ceaseless murmur of many waters.

This Hindu scroll was brought to Asia Minor about the Middle of the first century, having been given to Pol when he went to India about 46 A.D. to study the Hindu religion and be initiated in the Indian Mysteries ————————

SON OF PERFECTION - Part I - Prof. Hilton Hotema - printed covers
SON OF PERFECTION - Part II - Prof. Hotema - printed covers

October 11, 1971

GEORGE R. CLEMENTS, LL.B., LIT.D., N.D., D.C. (Deceased)

He became world famous under the Pseudonym (pen name) of Professor Hilton Hotema. We advertised Doctor Clements under this name for over twenty-five years. Because of his controversy with organized medicine and religion, he was under constant attack. He was finally barred from the use of the mails by the U.S. Postal Department. Thus he had to write his future books under another name.

The earlier works told too much of the truth on religion and the healing art. These were (now titled):

THE SECRET OF REGENERATION
THE GREAT LAW
ORTHOPATHY - co-authored by Dr. Herbert M. Shelton
THE DIVINE LIFE (Written over 40 years ago)
THE LAW OF LIFE AND HUMAN HEALTH

Dr. Clements was born in Fitchburg, Mass., February 7, 1878. His fore-fathers had a long life span. (See more of his early childhood, Spanish War years with photographs in his large book, LONG LIFE IN FLORIDA - 240 pages plus many additions

His son stated that his father passed away August 9, 1970, about 2:00 P.M., at the age of 92 years, 6 months and 2 days. This is all of the information we can secure from the family of the doctor. He had mentioned to us a few months previous that he felt 'light weighted' and could not seem to stay on earth. While he wanted to live to be 100 and write another book at that time, we believe that his work on this plane was finished and he was called to higher realms for more instruction.

Since we reside in California and Dr. Clements lived in Florida, we have no way of knowing further details. We did not communicate often - both being very active with our thousands of correspondents. There is absolutely no further information we can give.

Yours For Truth & Liberty,

HEALTH RESEARCH

The Art of Breathing —Aid to Health

By Gertrude Martin

The many wonderful inventions of the last century have enabled mankind to enter e new phase of development. The New Age is now upon us, and we cannot retreat; we must go forward. The Bible proclaims; "Behold"I make all things new." (Rev. 21:5). Therefore it is the duty of modern man to rebuild himself end to progress with the spirit of the time by adjusting himself to e better way of living in a changed world.

This is the age of nerves end brain. As e result of numerous labor-saving inventions the average man today hes to do little or no heavy physical work in order to earn his living. It is no longer muscles but brains that decide success in life. Our forefathers needed to develop strong muscles to be able to cope with the demands of their time. Our need today is to develop strong nerves end a god thinking capacity. Our predecessors could afford to eat hearty meals so as to develop strong muscles to fit themselves for heavy physical work. But to develop strong nerves and a virile brain - the deciding factors of modern life - it takes other methods than those required for strong muscles.

In our time we cannot afford to partake of heavy meals; instead we need lighter food, end - above all - deeper breathing because the nervous system, es well es the thinking capacity of the brain, depend more upon the breath we inhale than upon the food we eat. It is well known, for instance, that the electrons of the air ere necessary to sustain the ganglionic system. Indeed, the breath we take and the food we eat demand greater consideration today than ever before, as they are the fundamental needs pertaining to human life. These two elements decide man's physical well-being as well as his mental and spiritual development. For this reason the late Dr. Otoman Zar-Adusht He nish, the great reformer, philosopher, physician, and friend of all men, reminded his students to make the world "food-conscious" end also "breath-conscious." He taught e breathing technique that was helpful to those who were either sick or well. Two of his enlightening books which are known and read throughout the world are: Health and Breath Culture, and Diet and Cookery Book.

To a certain extent the world has become food-conscious; yet knowledge about proper food for man is still vague, and we have a long way to travel to reach the goal: "Perfect food for perfect man." Vegetarians are on the right road, and they are eager to do rightly, but even they often make mistakes as to proper combinations of food, end preparation and quantity of food to be consumed. Only our natural instinct is a reliable guide for selecting the right food for our well-being.

As a result of transgression of the natural laws of life, men today has lost his original intuition (instinct), and thus has gone astray. Animals, left to themselves, find the proper food suitable to each species. By instinct, a horse, a cow, a sheep or a goat is able to choose among all the herbs end grasses that grow in the meadow just what is good for itself.

The vital need for today is deeper breathing, for it will gradually restore to man his natural instinct. By deeper conscious inhalation, which brings inspiration, our instinct (intuition) will be regained. Then man need never ask: "What shall we eat? What shell we drink? How shall we act?" His natural intuition will safely guide him, and thereby he will do the right thing and choose the proper food. Thus will a great stride be made toward the goel and destiny of man.

The average man knows very little of the value of the atmosphere that surrounds him; nor of the priceless possibilities offered to him right here end now. As e rule, people know only that oxygen is contained in the air we breathe, that we inhale oxygen with every inhalation and that oxygen is necessary for the red blood corpuscles That is approximately all they know. They do not realize that more - a vast amount of vital substances; in fect, in the air that surrounds us can be found almost everything required for the sustenanc of the three-fold being of man - spirit, body, and mind. Dr. Ha'ni used to say: "We could live on breath alone if our lungs were better developed." All of the health and life-giving forces are contained in the universe (the atmospheric air), and it is for us to conscious ly draw more and more of these forces into our system by more though ful and deeper breathing. So far, science knows that the air contains: oxygen, nitrogen, hydrogen, zentrosoms, protons and electrons molecules, ether and atoms. These are all there--ready for us to take and to use freely (at no extra cost!). In the present Atomic Age we should become better acquainted with the powers of the universe, and learn how we may use them for our own well-being, progress and happiness.

The deplorable neglect of the lungs which are the dynamos of the whole body machine only can be explained by the utter ignorance of man concerning the importance of deeper breathing and the wonderful benefits he could derive from the life and health-giving forces of the universe.

Deeper breathing by inhalation and exhalation purifies the blood and assires its normal consistency.

Deeper breathing helps to restore a normal blood circulation.

Deeper breathing strengthens the nerves, the heart, and the thinking capacity of the brain.

Deeper breathing helps us in every way to a better, more conscious and improved life; for Breath is Life and Life is Breath.

We will realize our lack and how much we have neglected ourselves by pondering the fact that the lungs of every human being contain 800 millions of lung cells (alveoli), and that in the average man (according to medical examinations) only about 150-200 millions of lungs are active; approximately 600 millions of lung cells are absolutely wasted.

The first step in the direction of improved breathing, therefore, is to gradually increase the breathing capacity of the lungs and to train these organs toward fuller inhalations and deeper exhalations. By a few simple exercises, easily learned, in combination with hygienic care of the body, we soon will become more breath-conscious and accustomed to deeper and more effective breathing.

Here is a healthful hint on breathing: Sit erect (chest raised)
and relax all muscles of the body. Empty the lungs entirely by
deep exhalation. Remain breathless for three seconds, then inhale
deeply and exhale again as before. Repeat three to five times every
two hours in the daytime eo as to eliminate carbon-dioxide gas which
must not be allowed to accumulate in the system; auto-intoxication
is thus prevented. Be sure that all the muscles of the body are
relaxed while performing this simple exercise.

The late Dr. O. Z. A. Hanish, M.D., once declared: "Only the
breath we take in after a preceding thorough exhaletion is the right
one that brings to our lungs (and blood) ALL the vital elements--
ALL the chemicals of the universe, giving new life and strength to
all cells of the body."

Let us therefore remember to always exhale first and empty the
lungs to the utmost. Remain breathless for three seconds. Relax
all muscles of the body. Then inhale with a deep sobbing breath,
filling all parts of the lungs with the life-giving air.

There is always in our lungs some gaseous residue (waste) which,
first of ell, must be expelled before we start to inhale the fresh
air. Were we to start a breathing exercise with en inhalation, we
would invariably drew the waste matter deeper into our systems. Thi
is something to guard against. We would not drink a glass of water
that had been left standing overnight, but would first dispose of
the stale water, then fill the tumbler with fresh water and drink
it. So it is with our breath. We repeat: empty the lungs; get
rid of the waste matter, and so prepare the lungs for the inflow
of good fresh air. This is the reason why in the Mazdaznan Science
of Breath all breathing exercises ere to be started by a thorough
emptying of the lungs.

Concentration: For good results always concentrate on what you
are doing; when exhaling be fully aware or conscious of the gaseous
waste that you are expelling, and sense the immediate relief the
exhalation gives to the system; be sure you are relaxed. When inhaling think consciously of all the good that comes to you on "ether
waves," that is, all the oxygen for the red blood corpuscles, all
the electrons for the ganglion of the nervous system which go to
strengthen the nerves, all the atomic power for the benefit of your
whole being, and many more of God's blessings available for your
physical and mental development.

You should also follow in thought the inflow of the fresh air as
it enters the nostrils, the windpipe, the bronchial tubes, the air
sacks (alveoli), end from there finally entering the bloodstream.
Think of the whole process--consciously--and try to feel every phase
of inhalation and exhalation. Thought is a force that gives more
impetus to everything we do in our daily walks of life, and espec-
ially applicable to breath and breathing. Conscious breath and
conscious life are one and more than ever nseded in these troubled
times. Indeed the very essence of life is Breath and the Spirit
of God which we inhale together when breathing consciously. In
ancient Greece the word, "Pneuma," carried a duel meaning - both
"Spirit" and "Breath."

It is a fact that in Greece the power of breath was well known
and utilized. Breathing exercises also were practiced centuries

before in ancient Egypt. The knowledge of the power of breath for man's well-being and spiritual and mental development can be traced back even to the time of the great Zoroaster who lived approximately 7000 years B.C.

Many wise leaders of antiquity knew of the value of deep breathing. In those times, however, only priests and kings made use of the knowledge in order to obtain well-being, wisdom and inspiration to guide the people. In our present time man has forgotten his origin and his close relationship to God; indeed, he has failed to understand the very life principle--the atom--nor does he know much about instinct, inspiration, and intuition--all precious gifts from God to make life happier and healthier, more successful and peaceful. But all we have lost may be regained by re-established deeper and conscious breathing, by inhaling fully the "Cosmic Breat We are forever grateful to Dr. O. Z. A. Hanish who revived the wonderful knowledge regarding the power of breath, and who worked untiringly, lecturing all over the world, giving to all men this marvelous wisdom -- only for love. That knowledge -- thanks to him -- is no longer restricted to the few, but available to everyone.

Note: When inhaling we should be mindful always to inhale through the nose for the purpose of pre-warming, pre-moistening and pre-cleaning the inhaled air. The air passages inside the nose are not straight; they are twisted and turned. In this way nature intended to make certain that the inflowing air would be sufficiently prepared before it entered the lungs. It is wonderful to realiz that when man knows himself he begins to know God.

Exhalation practiced properly every two to three hours in the daytime for three minutes at a time cleanses the bloodstream and relieves the system by eliminating gaseous waste (carbon dioxide gas). We cannot prevent the formation of gaseous waste, as it is a result of metabolism, but we can prevent the accumulation of it and so prevent auto-intoxication by exhalation prolongations at the right time. For this reason the simple exercise as given herein is of immense value to us. In addition to purifying the blood, enhancing blood circulation, and enriching the blood, it also brings more lungcells into activity as exhalations and inhalations become longer and deeper.

Millions of minute cells are continuously at work within us to keep our body machines in good condition. Each cell has a special job to do for the benefit of the whole. Each cell has its own cell intelligence that directs the work. All body cells depend upon the bloodstream. By means of circulating through all parts of the body the blood brings to the cells all their necessary supplies, so enabling the cells to do their work. So far, so good; for so long as the blood is in a normal condition and there is good circulation all is well, and the cells are well supplied with all they need. Life processes can proceed harmoniously. Trouble begins only when, because of wrong feeding and insufficient breathing, the blood deteriorates (degenerates) and in consequence fails to supply the cells with their essential needs. Then the cells cannot perform properly, and as a result the whole body machine becomes out of order.

Now we all know that if we give proper fuel to our cars they wil run smoothly and efficiently. And how careful we ere in choosing the right oil and gas. But why do we not think more seriously about the machines --our bodies --which we use every day! Why do we not provide the best fuel-obtainable in the foods we eat and the breath we breathe.

It is true that blood "feeds," so to speak, each tiny cell of the body, but it is for us to see to it that the blood itself is well supplied with ell its needs to properly feed ell bodycells. Food and breath are responsible for the normal consistency of the blood, for its normally healthy condition end purity, free from poisons of ell kinds.

Let us follow the right course for our own good-partake of pure food and drink, and breathe the deep conscious breath. Let us take the food that is naturally meant for us, so kindly end abundantly offered by Nature's gardens and fields and found in God's own divine air.

Never forget that food and breath decide the quality of your blood, and that the quality of your blood decides the condition of the entire cell state of the body. There is no substitute for deeper breathing.

All cells benefit at once end all bodily processes receive new life as we breathe consciously end deeply. "The Fire of Life" burns brighter when more breath (air) permeates the body. To have acquired this vital information is most fortunate end valuable for ell of us who are interested in Life and Truth. Truth is always simple and easily understood. We were told this by Dr. Henish, a great teacher and friend of ell men, a learned doctor who brought to us these simple facts of life end the wondrous knowledge concerning the Power of Breath.

----- NEW EXERCISE -----

Training the lungs toward deeper breathing, gradually bringing more and more lungcells into activity end increasing the breath capacity of the lungs. Concentration, position and relaxation ere essential in all breathing exercises, as explained in the previous articles appearing in the DIGEST.

Empty the lungs, that is, breathe out gently but as much as possible without strain. Out, out, out.

Then fill the lungs to the count of two seconds and empty the lungs to the count of two seconds.

Inhale lungs to count of three seconds; exhale lungs to count of three seconds.

Inhale lungs to count of four seconds; exhale lungs to count of four seconds.

Inhale lungs to count of five seconds; exhale lungs to count of five seconds.

Inhale lungs to count of six seconds; exhale lungs to count of six seconds.

1957 The ancient fire philosophers taught the secret of the Flame Divine and knew the meaning of the Spark of Life. After fifty years of diligent research, Professor Hotema has dug from ancient ruins some fragments of ancient scriptures dealing with a marvelous secret of the Macrocosm. Included within this manuscript are discourses on The Flame Divine, Breath of Life, Union of the Astral and the Physical, as well as The Art of Breathing - Aid to Health by Gertrude Martin.